2005
CHILDREN'S MISSION YEARBOOK
for prayer & study

Sing to the LORD a new song —Ps. 96:1

The *2005 Children's Mission Yearbook for Prayer & Study* is published by Witherspoon Press and the Mission Education and Promotion (MEP) program team of Congregational Ministries Publishing, Congregational Ministries, a ministry of the General Assembly Council of the Presbyterian Church (U.S.A.). Sandra Moak Sorem is the publisher of Congregational Ministries Publishing.

Many people worked together to create this book. Christy Williams, director of Christian education, First Presbyterian Church, Tallassee, Florida, was the writer. The Rev. Dr. Eileen Lindner, deputy general secretary, National Council of the Churches of Christ in the U.S.A., contributed prayers for each week. Deborah Haines was the editor, Billie Healy the associate editor, Nancy Goodhue the copy editor, the Rev. Judy Hockenberry the children's curriculum liaison, Jeanne Williams the designer/art director, and the Rev. Jon Brown, senior editor/coordinator of MEP. Margaret Hall Boone, Carol E. Johnson, Lily Osuamkpe, Teresa Mader, Ivy Bell, and Mark Thomson also contributed to the *2005 Children's Yearbook.*

The cover for this book was designed by Carol Cornette of Louisville, Kentucky. Her inspiration came from the cover of the *2005 Mission Yearbook for Prayer & Study.* Carol also created all the illustrations inside the *Children's Yearbook.*

Where possible, the names of the people who took the photographs can be found on the pages where the photos appear. The Scripture verses for each week are usually part of the daily lectionary, taken from the *Book of Common Prayer,* with revisions that were made for inclusion in the *Lutheran Book of Worship.* Scripture quotations are from the New Revised Standard Version of the Bible, copyrighted 1989 by the Division of Christian Education of the National Council of the Churches of Christ in the U.S.A., and are used by permission.

Let us know what you think about the *2005 Children's Mission Yearbook for Prayer & Study*! Send a letter to The Editor, *Children's Mission Yearbook for Prayer & Study,* Mission Education and Promotion, Presbyterian Church (U.S.A.), 100 Witherspoon Street, Louisville, KY 40202-1396. Or send an e-mail to: dhaines@ctr.pcusa.org. Call us toll free at (888) 728-7228, ext. 5170.

You can order more copies of this book for your friends! Ask your minister, teacher, or parent to call (800) 524-2612 and ask for PDS #70-612-05-451. The cost is $5.50 each or $4.00 each for 10 or more.

A Message from the Stated Clerk

I really like to sing! I may not sing on pitch sometimes, but I still like to sing. I'm thinking about taking voice lessons one of these days. Will my friends ever be surprised!

I bet many of you like to sing, too. I bet many of you like to sing so much that you have joined a chorus at school or a choir at church. Isn't it fun to hear lots of different voices together, especially when they sing in harmony? Some sing the high notes, some sing the low ones, and others sing in the middle. If everyone sang just the low notes or just the high notes, we would be missing some beautiful music.

In many ways, the whole church is like a choir. All of us who follow Jesus are like the choir members. Just as in a choir we sing different notes, in the church we do different things to be helpful. We call it mission in the name of Jesus Christ. Some of us visit people who are sick. Some of us make sure that cans are recycled. Others of us tell stories of Jesus to people who have never heard them before.

In this book you will learn about all the many ways that Presbyterians are involved in mission. Some of us work side by side with others in mission here in the United States. Some of us work with our mission partners very far away in other countries. Together, we are like a choir—all singing different notes, but together making beautiful music. With our communities and partners we are all doing different kinds of mission. Together we are helping to make the world more like God created it to be.

I know you will do your special part to help! Have fun as you discover new friends in mission in the United States and around the world!

—Rev. Clifton Kirkpatrick, stated clerk, Office of the General Assembly

Suggestions for Using This Book

How you use your *Children's Mission Yearbook* depends on you. Every two pages cover one week in 2005. You might choose to do all of the activities for a week at one time. You might choose one activity to do each day until you have done them all in a week's time. You might choose to do the same activity each day. For example, we encourage you to pray each week's prayer every day. Some activities will take longer than a week to do. You will need an adult to help you with some activities, especially when you want to try one of the recipes! However you decide to use the book, we hope you will make it your own and learn as much as you can about being a Presbyterian and how Presbyterians are involved with mission all around the world. And, we hope that you have fun as you learn!

The Practice of Prayer

The Bible encourages believers to "pray without ceasing." This sounds impossible. Yet praying is like other disciplines: you have to keep at it, make a time to do it regularly, and keep interested in doing it. Throughout the pages of this book we have taken something from each week's stories to pray about. Many different forms of prayer are suggested. At first, it may not seem natural to pray in the ways suggested here. Maybe it will be easier to try these ways if you think about prayer as sharing your life with God—your thoughts, hopes, fears, feelings, and actions. The prayer sections of the *Children's Mission Yearbook* give you a chance to practice praying. Maybe through practicing different methods, you will find ways that mean something to you and that help you keep praying regularly.

Table of Contents

When you see this symbol, it means that you will be asked to explore the *Mission Yearbook for Prayer & Study* so that you can answer a question. Ask to borrow a copy from your pastor, teacher, or parent. Better yet, ask them to help you find the answers to the questions!

We are members of the Presbyterian Church (U.S.A.). The abbreviation for that is PC(USA), which is what we use in the book. Another abbreviation we use is Rev., which means Reverend. That's the title we use for ministers, as in the Rev. Susan Church.

MISSION IN THE UNITED STATES

Presbytery of Kiskiminetas

Pennsylvania

The inmates at Pine Grove Prison, a state correctional facility in Indiana, Pennsylvania, eagerly await their Christmas Day visit from the Presbyterians. The Presbytery of Kiskiminetas involves members of churches within the presbytery on a prison task force that provides gifts to inmates. Can you find the Presbytery of Kiskiminetas on the map on page 112? The people on this task force enjoy buying gifts for the inmates at Pine Grove. They see that a small gift given by someone who believes in God's grace can make a difference in a person's life. Gifts include chocolate candies and cakes that are not usually available to prisoners.

Going in the jail, even as a volunteer, can be scary. Volunteers must complete lots of forms and be cleared of having a criminal history before they can be admitted. After that they can enter the jail. The steel doors clang shut, and the volunteer is "behind bars." Those involved in the presbytery's prison task force are willing to be a little nervous in order to be instruments of Christ's grace to those in jail. Giving gifts and spending time visiting and praying with inmates are ways these volunteers say to them that God loves them and is with them.

Giving What You Have

Make a New Year's resolution to pray and care for someone outside your family throughout the year. You may choose one of the mission co-workers from your presbytery or community to write to and send care packages to throughout the year. If you don't think you can keep up with this resolution on your own, ask your family to help you. Maybe you can all take turns writing to the person and include the person in family mealtime prayers together.

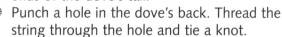

Scripture

O sing to the LORD a new song; sing to the LORD, all the earth (Psalm 96:1).

Craft

Peace Dove

The dove is often used as a symbol of peace. In this New Year, give someone the gift of peace by making him or her this reminder of God's peace.

Materials

scissors
1 piece of string at least 12 inches long (any color)
1 piece of white or blue thin paper (like what you would use in a computer printer)
1 piece of cardstock or poster-board paper (blue or white works best)
markers and a pencil
tape
hole punch

Instructions

✳ Cut one of the thin pieces of paper in half as shown.
✳ Fold both halves of paper like an accordion.
✳ On the piece of cardstock or poster board, draw a bird's body (like a thick banana) lightly with a pencil. Cut out the body.
✳ At the center of the body and at the back end of the body, cut two small slits (an adult may have to help you).
✳ Slip one of the accordion-folded pieces of paper into the bird's body at the center slit and one in the end slit. Gently fan out the accordion folds so the wings and tail are full. You may want to tape together the two ends of the dove's tail.
✳ Punch a hole in the dove's back. Thread the string through the hole and tie a knot.
✳ Draw eyes on the dove, and on its back write "A Gift of Peace."

MISSION AROUND THE WORLD

Vietnam

Look at the world map on pages 110–111 and find Vietnam. For many people in our country, Vietnam is a place they came to know through a war. In the past 25 years Vietnam has worked hard to change its image from a place of war to a place where people are peacefully thriving.

Church World Service (CWS), a partner of the PC(USA), is an international relief and assistance agency that originally went to Vietnam to help restore basic housing, safe water, and adequate food. Soon CWS volunteers realized that their efforts were better spent working as partners with the Vietnamese as they worked to rebuild and establish human rights for all the people.

One such partnership is with Principal Nguyen Thi Hai's boarding school for ethnic minorities located in Vietnam's mountains. To get to the school a person must cross a bamboo bridge, then hike a mile up a dirt path. Since it would take at least a day's journey for most students to get there, they live at the school full time. Most students are from poor farming families. For years the school lacked things it needed. Church World Service has provided mosquito netting, warm blankets, clothing, and books for the library. In the past someone had to haul water from a long distance just to cook. Now a new well in the school's courtyard provides safe water for cooking, drinking, and even bathing!

Many of the students are girls, even though many Vietnamese still believe girls shouldn't be educated. In Vietnam 70 percent of those who cannot read are female. The school encourages the girls who are students to invite other girls from their villages to consider attending school. Through partnerships such as this one between CWS and the boarding school, the Vietnamese are finding peace, hope, and life returning to their country.

The crane is an ancient Asian symbol of peace and long life. During the war in Vietnam cranes fled the country, but today as Vietnam rebuilds, they are returning home.

Prayer

Dear God, in this New Year I thank you for those who travel to other countries to serve and tell your story. Keep them in your care. Be with the inmates at Pine Grove Prison and the students in Vietnam. In Jesus' name. Amen.

Did You Know?

Did you know the stated clerk of the General Assembly for the whole Presbyterian Church (U.S.A.) is the Rev. Dr. Clifton Kirkpatrick? Did you read his special message to you on page 2? You can find another message from him about Palm Sunday in the *2005 Mission Yearbook for Prayer & Study.*

What You Can Do

Ask your pastor to find out who in your presbytery or community is serving in the military or as a mission co-worker overseas or in another state. Make some lightweight bookmarks using the Scripture verse for this week. Send these bookmarks with a note to these people and let them know you are praying for and thinking about them. Then spend some time praying for each of the persons to whom you wrote.

Word of the Week

Gift

A gift is something given to someone freely. It can also be a talent. When someone has the gift of singing, he or she can sing beautifully. The Presbyterians who work at Pine Grove Prison have the gift of giving: they have a talent for giving gifts to others!

MISSION IN THE UNITED STATES
Presbytery of Carlisle
Pennsylvania

A small group of young men sit in a Presbyterian church in Harrisburg, Pennsylvania, which is within the Presbytery of Carlisle. (Find this presbytery on the map on page 112.) Together they have traveled from Sudan to Ethiopia, to Kenya, and to the United States with a dream of completing their educations and finding a safe place to live. As children these young men were separated from their parents during a civil war in Sudan. Not knowing where to turn for help, they banded together and walked from Sudan to Ethiopia, where they stayed in a refugee camp. When it got too dangerous to live in Ethiopia, they walked back to Sudan. Again they had to leave Sudan, and they walked to a refugee camp in Kenya. After living several years in Kenya, their journey ended in the United States. Look at the map on pages 110–111. Find Sudan. Trace your finger over to Ethiopia, then through Sudan to Kenya. How many miles do you think they walked?

These boys, now grown into young men, were able to get immigration papers to the United States while in the refugee camp in Kenya. All had a dream of getting an education and training. For nine years in the refugee camp in Kenya these young men lived in grass-roofed huts or tents. In Harrisburg they live amid computers, cell phones, and cars. Each one is realizing his dream of finishing school. The young men believed that all along their long journey God had provided for their needs. God gave them hope that they would one day live into their dream. With support from the people in the Presbytery of Carlisle, God continues to provide for these young men who seem to have found a home and a new beginning.

Did You Know?
In 2003, the PC(USA) had 463 mission workers serving in 71 countries. Among these workers were 352 long-term mission workers.

Scripture

Jesus said to them, "I am the bread of life. Whoever comes to me will never be hungry, and whoever believes in me will never be thirsty" (John 6:35).

Dr. Cynthia Morgan and Shalony's mother, Monica, are happy Shalony is doing well.

Recipe
Chicken and Cauliflower

Many recipes from Bangladesh include curry. Try this recipe without adding the chicken breasts for a vegetarian meal or with the chicken for a tasty poultry dish.

Ingredients
1/4 cup lentils
1 can chicken broth, heated
4 cooked boneless chicken breasts
1 cup chopped onion
1/4 head of cauliflower cut into pieces
1 cup grated carrots
1/2 cup chopped celery
1 8-oz. can of tomato sauce
1 tsp. curry powder

Cook lentils according to bag instructions. Add the vegetables to the lentils. Slice the chicken breasts and add to the vegetable and lentil mixture. Stir in the tomato sauce and curry powder. Cook for an additional 30 minutes on a low heat. Serve over rice.

MISSION AROUND THE WORLD

Bangladesh

Bangladesh is a country with a rich heritage in art and architecture. Find it on the map on page 111. The people of Bangladesh produce beautiful cotton textiles. Even with its deep heritage and resources, Bangladesh is a poor country. Many towns have no medical facilities, and many existing hospitals do not have the equipment or resources to care for babies who are born prematurely.

Shalony was almost born in the town where her parents lived. But her mother, Monica, became very ill three months before Shalony was supposed to be born. The town where Shalony's family lived had a hospital, but the hospital did not have an intensive care for newborns and premature babies. So Monica was rushed to the Christian Mission Hospital in Rajshahi, where Shalony was born weighing only two and a half pounds. Because she was born so early, her little body had not fully developed to do all the things a normal newborn baby can do, including drinking milk. For six weeks Shalony stayed in the hospital while the hospital staff worked with her. After six weeks her body had grown and developed enough that she could go home with her mother. She weighed four pounds, still much lighter than most babies at birth, but she could drink. Cynthia Morgan, the physician at the hospital who took care of Shalony and a PC(USA) mission co-worker, wrote, "Indeed, here in Bangladesh, God has lifted the lowly and has filled the hungry with good things!"

Giving What You Have

How many hospitals are in the town, city, or community where you live? For each one, put 10 cents in the offering plate on Sunday.

Prayer

Hold a single slice of bread. Any kind will do—white bread, pita, tortillas. Study the bread. It is so basic and such ordinary food we forget that without it there would be no sandwiches, no French toast, nothing to soak up gravy! Jesus said he was the bread of life because he is so basic to our lives and gives us the strength to live. Still looking at the bread, pray silently for those who do not have bread today. Tell God how it makes you feel to know about hungry people in places like Bangladesh. Share with God what you hope for people who are hungry and try to make one promise to God about how you can help.

Word of the Week   Hope

Having a desire for something
Opening your heart
Praying for a particular thing or event
Excitement, expectation

Can you find all the mission workers living in Bangladesh and Sudan? Look in Appendix B in the back of the Mission Yearbook for Prayer & Study and figure it out!

What You Can Do

Throughout this resource you will read the terms *mission partners* and *mission workers* or *co-workers*. Find out what Presbyterian mission co-workers do and who they are. Ask a parent or caregiver to help you find the PC(USA) Web site, www.pcusa.org. Select "U.S. & World Mission," and under "In the World" click on "Letters from Mission Workers" to find out where we have mission workers. Who are mission partners? Spend some time browsing through the denomination's Web site. If you don't have Internet access, see if your pastor has a *2005 Mission Yearbook for Prayer & Study* that you might borrow. This resource will tell you more about mission partners, mission workers, and mission projects in our country and around the world.

MISSION IN THE UNITED STATES
Presbytery of Philadelphia
Pennsylvania

If you walk down a city block in West Philadelphia you may notice that the buildings are old and people's resources seem limited. However, in this area of the city the community is alive and energized. The spirit behind this renewal can be credited to the West Philly Five, five African American churches located in this area that were able to see beyond their community's limitations and look toward their neighbors' rich diversity and lively spirits. Each congregation realized its membership was aging, attendance was down, buildings were in need of repair, and money was limited. Rather than closing their doors, these churches joined together to bring renewal.

Two of the churches' favorite projects are the West Philly Five's Youth Choir and the Friday night

Scripture

Even youths will faint and be weary, and the young will fall exhausted; but those who wait for the LORD shall renew their strength, they shall mount up with wings like eagles, they shall run and not be weary, they shall walk and not faint (Isaiah 40:29–31).

Youth Hour of Power. Combining voices from all five churches, the youth choir sings at a different one of the five churches every Sunday. The Youth Hour of Power reaches out to include neighbors who may not be attending church. Local youth rappers, dancers, poets, and praise singers come out for the Friday night music, and the community is alive with the beat of God's good news.

Find the Presbytery of Philadelphia on the map on page 112.

Puzzle
Who Needs My Help?

The people below at times need our help, our prayers, and God's renewal. Unscramble the words in the "alphabet soup" to find out who they are.

1. hessomel
2. ugeefer
3. dowwi
4. reignhob
5. difern
6. wridowe
7. tapren
8. rucchh
9. snimios orkwer
10. tisser
11. therrbo

1. _____
2. _____
3. _____
4. _____
5. _____
6. _____
7. _____
8. _____
9. _____
10. _____
11. _____

Answers: 1. homeless, 2. refugee, 3. widow, 4. neighbor, 5. friend, 6. widower, 7. parent, 8. church, 9. mission worker, 10. sister, 11. brother

What You Can Do

In one month, on February 6, a major sports event occurs: the Super Bowl. Start planning now to participate in this year's Souper Bowl of Caring and help families in need in your community. Call 1-800-358-SOUP or go to www.souperbowl.org to get detailed information. Talk to your church school teacher, youth adviser, or pastor and ask your church's session if your church can participate in this event. Advertise by doing a minute for mission or putting information about the Souper Bowl offering in your newsletter and on bulletin boards. Gather some friends together and some good deep pots and get ready to do a Souper project!

Did You Know?

In 1990 members of a Presbyterian youth group in Columbia, South Carolina, were upset at how much money was spent on the Super Bowl for advertising, tickets, and refreshments. They thought instead of just watching the game, they could be making a difference in someone's life. After the service on Super Bowl Sunday they stood outside their church's sanctuary with large pots asking parishioners to make donations, then took the money to the local soup kitchen. Thus began the first Souper Bowl of Caring.

Giving What You Have

Count how many commercials are shown on a TV program you watch. For each one, save 10 cents to put in the Souper Bowl collection on February 6.

Word of the Week   Renewal

When we are renewed we are given new energy and a clear direction. When a church is renewed it finds a new and exciting direction to serve God.

Prayer

God of creation, on days when I feel small and as if everything is going wrong, help me. Be with me especially on those days and help me to remember you and the promises Jesus made that you would always be close at hand. Help me recall that you made me for life and love and that I too can gain the strength of eagles and soar with your grace and presence to guide me. Amen.

MISSION AROUND THE WORLD

Republics of Central Asia

The writer of Psalm 137 asks, "How could we sing the Lord's song in a foreign land?" For many in Turkmenistan, Uzbekistan, and Kazakhstan the question was, "How do we sing the Lord's song in our *own* land?" For decades the governments of these countries had silenced the songs and expressions of faith. Even speaking the name of God was forbidden. Maybe for you it is difficult to imagine living in a place where you were not allowed to express your faith or practice your religion. Fortunately, for many of these Central Asian countries, religious restrictions are becoming more relaxed. But many of the people are poor. One church worker explains it by saying that mission workers have two main jobs to work on in Central Asia. One of the jobs is to make sure that everyone has enough food to eat. The other job is to teach the people of Central Asia about the amazing love of God. Jesus refers to himself as the "bread of life." People need both bread that will make their bodies strong and God's love, which will make them strong enough to face their daily struggles. The mission partners who work with these people are helping them grow in their minds, bodies, and spirits.

A Central Asian boy carries bread baked by his mother for sale along the street.

MISSION IN THE UNITED STATES

Cimarron Presbytery

Oklahoma

Imagine you were told that you had to make your own school clothes! If you weren't already interested in sewing, you probably wouldn't be happy. For the high school students in Gatundu Presbytery in Kenya, sewing school uniforms is helping them go to school.

Several years ago the Cimarron Presbytery in Oklahoma made contact with the Gatundu Presbytery in Kenya. Find Cimarron Presbytery on the map on page 112 and Kenya on the map on page 111. The two presbyteries enjoyed learning about one another, praying for each other, and supporting one another in ministries. Last year the people in Cimarron Presbytery decided they wanted to meet their friends in Kenya and help with a project that would give local Kenyans job possibilities and

Scripture

Speaking the truth in love, we must grow up in every way into . . . Christ (Ephesians 4:15).

would help the education of the children as well. The Gatundu group was concerned about the cost of sending children to school beyond the primary grades. The two presbyteries chose to work with a local center to teach sewing skills and make school uniforms. The sewing center now provides training to high school students and gives them a skill they can use throughout their lives. The work also helps to pay for their school fees so they may continue going to school. The students are empowered by their new skills. Without the sewing center many of these students' families would not be able to afford for them to stay at school. The Cimarron Presbytery works with the Gatunda Presbytery to buy materials for the center and to give instruction to the students.

Craft

3-D Weaving

Both India and Africa are known for their beautiful cloth and weavings. Try out a vibrant 3-D weaving of your own design.

Materials

1 9-inch square of foam board (preferably in a dark color. If it is white, cut a piece of solid dark fabric, glue it to the foam board, and let it dry.)

small, thin nails (or you can experiment by using clear plastic-topped thumb tacks)

different colored threads (embroidery thread works fine too)

pencil

sheet of paper

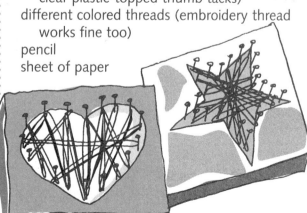

Decide on a design for your weaving. Choose something simple like a star, diamond, or heart. Draw a pattern on a piece of paper and place it on the foam board. Poke the small nails (or tacks) through the paper into the foam board along the lines of your pattern. Nails should be placed between 1/2 inch and 1 inch from each other. Carefully tear off the pattern when the nails (tacks) are in place.

Choose a nail at one end of the pattern to be your starting point. Choose a color of thread and tie it to the nail. Begin weaving the thread by going across the pattern and wrapping the thread around any nail. Then bring the thread back across the pattern, randomly wrapping it around a different nail. Keep moving from nail to nail in this manner. Do not pull too tightly or you will pull out the nails. You can reuse nails and you can go from side to side. The point is to fill in the pattern with colors of thread. By the end you will want to have used each nail. When you have finished with that color, tie it to a nail and cut off any excess thread. Choose a new color and after tying one end to a nail, begin weaving again. Use as many colors as you want.

Prayer

God of everyone, we pray that all Christians everywhere may remember that we are all really one church under Christ's leadership. Help us to think and act like we are all your people and not think so much about our differences. In Jesus' name. Amen.

Kenyan school children show their excitement about the new sewing project.

What You Can Do

Is there someone you know, like a little sister or brother, whom you could empower in some way? You could teach her or him how to do something new like tie shoelaces or learn a new word.

Giving What You Have

You may not have to wear school uniforms, but you do have to use school books! How many school books do you have this year? For each one, put 10 cents in the offering plate on Sunday.

Did You Know?

The Week of Prayer for Christian Unity begins on Tuesday, January 18. During this week Christians of all denominations, like Presbyterians, Catholics, and Methodists, pray that all churches can put aside differences and be together in Christ.

MISSION AROUND THE WORLD
India

An old proverb says:

Give a person a fish and he or she will eat today. Teach a person to fish and he or she will eat tomorrow too.

Scott and Melanie Smith are mission co-workers in India. Find India on the map on page 111. Scott works with the Emmanuel Hospital Association, an organization that works to help communities. Scott and Melanie have worked hard to convince others in the association that the proverb about giving someone a fish or teaching someone to fish is true. When Scott and Melanie first arrived in India, the way of helping the community people was to give them what they needed. Scott and Melanie are training the people of the community so that they will not have to ask for help but will be able to help themselves. They want the people to be empowered. Scott says that the projects they do, like irrigation work, adult education, and crafts, are the ways in which they can teach the villagers to gain more control over their own lives. When the people of the community are able to use their skills and abilities, the quality of their lives will be enriched.

Word of the Week

Empowered

When we are empowered, we are stronger inside ourselves and have more control over our own lives and decisions. Some people are pushed down all the time by the things that happen in their lives and in their community or country. When those people are empowered, they are lifted up and able to have a strong voice in what happens in their life.

MISSION IN THE UNITED STATES

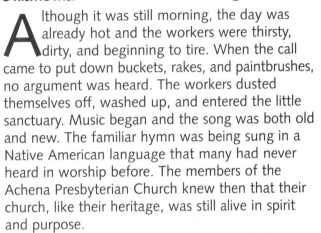

Indian Nations Presbytery

Oklahoma

Although it was still morning, the day was already hot and the workers were thirsty, dirty, and beginning to tire. When the call came to put down buckets, rakes, and paintbrushes, no argument was heard. The workers dusted themselves off, washed up, and entered the little sanctuary. Music began and the song was both old and new. The familiar hymn was being sung in a Native American language that many had never heard in worship before. The members of the Achena Presbyterian Church knew then that their church, like their heritage, was still alive in spirit and purpose.

The Achena Church is one of several Native American congregations within the boundaries of the Indian Nations Presbytery in Oklahoma. Find this presbytery on the map on page 112. Over the past decade, the church had lost many members. Faced with the possibility of having to close, the church, with support from the presbytery, wrote a proposal to improve their grounds and build a new fellowship hall. On this particular day members from churches all over the presbytery were clearing overgrown brush, cleaning up old buildings, repainting the sanctuary, and freshening up furniture. The hymn that began worship that morning was new because the language was unfamiliar to many present. The hymn was also new because it represented a new spirit of partnership among the churches in the presbytery. All were feeling blessed that morning.

Did You Know?

When Europeans first arrived in the Americas, there were close to 1,000 Native American languages spoken. Today only about 700 are still spoken. Native-language speakers are aging and dying and few young people are learning to speak their native languages.

Scripture

May *God be gracious to us and bless us and make God's face to shine upon us* (Psalm 67:1).

Recipe

Modified Vegetable Momo

Cooking in Nepal includes many spices and herbs that we cannot always get in this country. Try this dish from Nepal with several changes to make it easier to cook in your kitchen.

Vegetable momo is usually a kind of vegetable dumpling. In this version, it is more of a "bread pocket." If you would prefer to make this a dumpling, rather than baking the rolls in the oven, try steaming them for about 8 minutes.

Ingredients

1 container of refrigerator crescent rolls
1/2 stick of butter, softened
3 cups of assorted vegetables (fresh or canned vegetables. Carrots, green peas, corn, and green beans work best.)
1 red pepper, finely chopped
1 small onion, finely chopped
1 tsp. garlic, finely chopped
1/2 tsp. ground ginger
1/2 tsp. ground black pepper
1/4 cup chopped cilantro
1 cup shredded sharp cheddar cheese

Roll out refrigerator crescent rolls. Separate into triangles. Rinse or steam vegetables. Using 1/2 stick of butter, lightly brown the onion in a skillet. Add the red pepper, garlic, black pepper, and vegetables. Stir-fry until vegetables are slightly soft. Let cool a little.

Spoon some of the vegetable mixture into each wide end of the triangles of crescent rolls. Sprinkle some of the cheese on top. Roll up crescent roll gently, closing up the sides by pinching the dough together. Cook in an oven following instructions on crescent roll package.

MISSION AROUND THE WORLD

Nepal

Haejung and Simon Park are PC(USA) mission co-workers serving in Kathmandu, Nepal. Can you find Nepal on the map on page 111? Haejung works in a hospital. One day she noticed that the staff in the hospital's children's room were not always enthusiastic. Haejung thought an extra helper would be good. She asked Gita, a young woman who helped her and her husband with household chores, to go with her to the hospital. When Gita arrived at the children's room, her eyes twinkled and her face brightened. She began caring for the children, assisting in their medical treatment, sharing hopes and concerns with their parents, and teaching the children the importance of discipline and responsibility. Soon after Gita began her work at the hospital, she met Ambika, a five-year-old girl whose legs were paralyzed. Ambika had no family to visit her. She had been abandoned at the hospital. In time, Gita became Ambika's main caregiver. Gita knit Ambika caps and socks, brought her clothes from home, and exercised her legs to help circulate her blood.

Simon Park writes, "We are blessed to be a part of Gita's joy. Gita is blessed to be able to give. Ambika is blessed by the loving care, and we know God is blessed by the love we share."

Church elders apply fresh paint to the Achena Fellowship Hall in Oklahoma.

Word of the Week
Blessed

When we are blessed we feel happy and thankful for things we see have come from God. Usually we feel blessed when we receive things or have things that we do not feel we earned but which are given to us with love and grace.

What You Can Do

Ambika was alone in the hospital until Gita visited her and became her friend. Are there people in your church who are lonely? Ask your parents, church school teacher, pastor, or older friend if you could go along with them to visit someone who could use a friend.

Giving What You Have

In what ways do you feel blessed? What people or things bless your life? Put 5 cents in the offering plate on Sunday for each blessing you think of.

Prayer

Go for a short walk. See if you can think of a joy or blessing for each step you take. As you walk thank God for each blessing. When you have shared with God all the blessings you can think of, turn around and start to walk back. Think now of how these blessings make you happy and how you might share your happiness with others.

Scripture

MISSION IN THE UNITED STATES

Presbytery of Tres Rios

Texas

The Presbytery of Tres Rios may be small in number of churches, but it has a BIG vision for ministry. With only 35 churches this presbytery in western Texas spans hundreds of miles of the Texas border with Mexico. With Mexico so close, it seems neighborly to work as partners for peace and justice. Pasos de Fe is located in Cuidad Juarez, Mexico, just across the border from El Paso, Texas, which is in the Presbytery of Tres Rios. Pasos de Fe is also one of seven Border Ministries sponsored by the PC(USA). Mission groups of youth and adults from churches all over the country come to help with building projects and social programs.

The Presbytery of Tres Rios is also hard at work across the border in the United States. Project Vida, a social service ministry, provides medical, dental, educational, housing, and job training services to people living in a low-income neighborhood of El Paso. Further away in Midland, the Presbytery of Tres Rios and three nearby Presbyterian churches support a preschool program for low-income children called St. Andrew's Mission. Parents pay $5 a week for a good place to leave their children while they work. The mission also provides an after-school program for children in elementary school. Families can get things from the clothing and food closet. In the most eastern corner of the presbytery, Project Dignidad gives out food and clothing to people in need in the San Angelo area. Project Dignidad also offers counseling and assistance in paying bills.

From east to west, north and south, the Presbytery of Tres Rios is seeking to attend to the needs of its neighbors in the name of Christ. Find this presbytery on the map on page 112.

"If any want to become my followers, let them deny themselves and take up their cross and follow me. For those who want to save their life will lose it, and those who lose their life for my sake, and for the sake of the gospel, will save it"

(Mark 8:34–35).

A child attends preschool at St. Andrew's Mission in Midland, Texas.

Giving What You Have

Think of something you can do or give that would be a small sacrifice for you. It could be letting a brother or sister watch a favorite TV show rather than your favorite show or putting aside money to give to the Souper Bowl next week (see page 17).

Did You Know?

In 1870 a teacher, Melinda Rankin, moved her school from Brownsville, Texas, across the Rio Grande River to Matamoras, Mexico. Melinda was the first Protestant missionary to enter Mexico.

MISSION AROUND THE WORLD

Malaysia

Turn to page 111 and locate Malaysia on the map. For several years Malaysia was doing well, but in 2001 the economy of Malaysia suffered greatly. Paul Friesen, a PC(USA) mission co-worker in Malaysia, has been touched by the sacrifices and openness of many of the people he has met there. He writes about a retired school worker who gave up a well-paying job as a school principal just two years before he could have retired. Lye Chew reached out to students from other countries and often had them in his home but found it difficult to do so with all he had to do as a principal. So, even though he was close to retirement, Lye Chew asked to be transferred to a middle school as a teacher. In this new job, Lye Chew and his family were able to spend more time with students. The family invited students to their home for meals, often cooking food that students would know from their home country. The Chews led discussions about God and religion. Mr. Chew presented the life and teachings of Jesus as part of these groups. Slowly and with love, the Chews showed Christ's love through their actions. Lye Chew's sacrifice of position did not make him wealthy but did bring the richness of God's love to his family and to the international students in his school.

What You Can Do

Check the date of your newest world atlas or globe. If it is five years old or older, ask your parents to replace it with a new one. The world has been rapidly changing. Keep the atlas or globe in a place where you can get to it easily. When you hear or read about a place in school, look it up. When you use this resource, check locations on your atlas or globe and on the map on pages 110–111 of this book.

Prayer

Faithful God, give me strength so that I can keep the promises that I have made to you, to myself, and to others. When I forget what I have said I'll do, bring me back to my promise and help me to help others. Amen.

Puzzle

Sacrifice Word Hunt

Find as many words as possible using the letters in the word of the week. Words must have more than two letters. (Suggestion: write the letters on paper and cut them apart to help you find letter combinations.)

SACRIFICE

Word of the Week Sacrifice

To sacrifice is to give up something very important to us. What sacrifice did Lye Chew make in the story about Malaysia?

MISSION IN THE UNITED STATES

Presbytery of Grand Canyon

Arizona

The people in Arizona's Presbytery of Grand Canyon are offering hope and helping others. Find this presbytery on the map on page 112. Morning Star is a new church development in Surprise, Arizona. A new church development is a new church that for a few years gets some help from the presbytery, the synod, and the General Assembly as it is growing until it can stand on its own. Even though Morning Star is still getting help, it is reaching out as a partner to a cooperative in Kenya that makes beads and beadwork handicrafts. Church members sell the handicrafts in the United States and then send the money that is made back to the cooperative to help pay the school fees for girls in the village. Without the money to help them stay in school, these girls would have a difficult life.

Another church, Tuba City Presbyterian Church, is one of the oldest in the presbytery and is part of the Navajo Nation. In recent years the church began to lose members. Creative thinkers in the congregation came up with the idea of opening a thrift store and using the profits to help the church stay open and able to support itself. Other churches in the presbytery support the church by collecting items to be sold in the thrift store. Currently the church is open, and both it and the store are doing well. Throughout the presbytery church members are helping each other as they spread the good news of God's love.

What You Can Do

If your church has an Ash Wednesday service, see if your family can attend it. Think about things you might want to do during Lent. You may want to give up something, like drinking sodas, or you may want to do something kind for someone else. Spend some time thinking if there are some ways you want to do things differently.

Scripture

Create in me a clean heart, O God, and put a new and right spirit within me (Psalm 51:10).

Craft

Valentines

Valentine's Day is next week. Rather than spending extra money on valentines for your friends and family this year, spend some time making very special notes to tell people that you care.

On construction paper (any color) trace and then cut out your handprint. Be sure to cut in between each finger. Using another piece of construction paper, cut out a small heart. Glue it onto the center of your handprint's palm. Fold down the middle and ring fingers on your handprint and glue down. This is the American Sign Language symbol for "I love you." In the small heart, write your valentine's message.

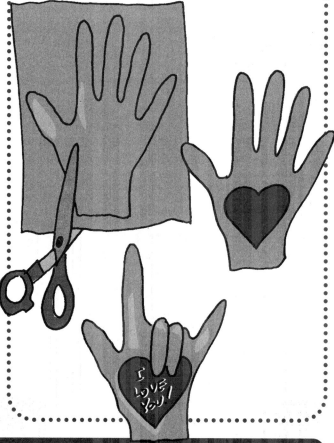

Word of the Week
Lent

Lent is the church season that comes right before Easter. It starts on Ash Wednesday, which happens this week. Lent is the forty days before Easter, not counting Sundays.

MISSION AROUND THE WORLD
Pakistan

Do you know that there is a Presbyterian Church in Pakistan? We usually think of Pakistan as a country of Muslim citizens—and with 97 percent of the country being Muslim, that would be a good guess. The remaining 3 percent of the country's citizens are Christian or Hindu. Though small, the Presbyterian Church of Pakistan and its mission co-workers in the country are active in bringing the love of Jesus Christ to both refugees and citizens. Find Pakistan on the map on page 112. Joseph and Shanthi Rajanesan are PC(USA) mission co-workers working with the Presbyterian Church of Pakistan. Joseph directs the Thal Project, which helps villages in the Thal Desert with their farming. Many people who had no land or homes came to live in the Thal Desert in the 1950s after irrigation canals were built that brought water to the land. Now the Thal Project has tractors for the people to use to plow their land. It provides farmers with seeds and other things they need at a fair price.

Joseph Rajanesan (on the right) helps residents of the Thal Desert with their farming.

Prayer

Dear God, give strength to those who are helping the villages in the Thal Desert with their farming so that they might be able to grow enough food. Bless the members of Morning Star and Tuba City Presbyterian as they reach out to others. Amen.

Giving What You Have

February 6 is the date for the Souper Bowl of Caring, a program started by young people from Spring Valley Presbyterian Church in Columbia, South Carolina. It is called the Souper Bowl because it is held on the same day as a football championship, the Super Bowl. It reminds us that there are people in every country who do not have much more to eat than a bowl of soup. Count the number of cans of soup your family has and give 25 cents for each one to your congregation's Souper Bowl of Caring offering.

Did You Know?

Lent at first was a time of preparation for people who were going to be baptized. It has become a time for Christians to think about their lives and ways they want to do better. Some Christians will fast during Lent, which means they go without eating anything during part of the day. Others will think of things to give up during Lent to help them remember Christ's sacrifice of his life. It's also a time for giving to and doing things for people who are in need. Lent starts with Ash Wednesday, and many Christians go to services during which ashes are put on their foreheads.

MISSION IN THE UNITED STATES

Presbytery de Cristo

The temperature is well over 100 degrees and there is no shade. Armed guards watch the steel wall that separates one town from another. Sometimes it seems extreme to spend so much effort to keep one town away from another. Towns are just places where people live and people are a lot alike. But a wall and a border patrol separate the people in Arizona and New Mexico from the people in Sonora, Mexico. In the past few years, hundreds of people from Mexico have passed through Sonora every day trying to leave Mexico and enter the United States. They leave Mexico to find better work opportunities and living conditions. The U.S. government has cracked down on these border crossings. The churches within the Presbytery de Cristo have been challenged about how to respond to both the border patrol and the migrants wishing to enter the country. In the past three years over 1,000 people have died in their attempts to enter the United States because they have so far to walk and don't carry enough water and food. Many are children and teenagers.

The presbytery has responded to these migrants by supporting two Presbyterian Border Ministries within their bounds, Frontera de Cristo and Campaneros en Mission. These ministries make life on the Mexican border more bearable for the people who live there. In addition, several churches in the presbytery support a group called Humane Borders, which has set up water stations along the routes taken by immigrants. Another group supported by churches is called Samaritans. Its volunteers travel in Jeeps and assist migrants who are having a hard time walking across the desert. The members of the Presbytery de Cristo have a vision of a better world for their neighbors, the migrants.

Scripture

"For God so loved the world that God gave his only Son, so that everyone who believes in him may not perish but may have eternal life" (John 3:16).

Recipe
Southwestern Sub Sandwich
Ingredients

1 can black beans
1 can red kidney beans
1 can corn
8 oz. salsa (mild to hot, you can decide)
4 oz. plain yogurt
1/2 cup mayonnaise
1 small chopped onion (optional)
1 loaf French bread or hoagie rolls
1 cup shredded cheddar cheese
butter

Empty the cans of black beans, kidney beans, and corn into a strainer and rinse with cold water. Cut the French bread into 6-inch sections and then slice open, or open the hoagie rolls if you are using them. Lightly butter both sides of the open sections and sprinkle on some shredded cheese. Put in a toaster oven and lightly melt the cheese and brown the bread. In a medium-sized bowl mix the salsa, yogurt, and mayonnaise. Add the bean and corn mixture and onion. Mix gently but well. Remove bread from the toaster oven and spoon bean mixture on the bread. Serve with tortilla chips. Yum!

Giving What You Have

The One Great Hour of Sharing offering is received by most churches on Easter, which is March 27 this year. If your church has coin boxes for this offering, use one this week to start saving for the offering.

MISSION AROUND THE WORLD

Indonesia

Indonesia is made up of a group of islands north of Australia. Find it on the map on page 111. Most of the people of Indonesia are Muslim, and only about 8 percent of the population is Christian. In the last few years people of both religions have fought each other. Bernie and Farsijana Risakotta-Adeney are PC(USA) mission co-workers who are working to bring peace among the people of Indonesia. They have taught pastors all over the country about what happens when religion is used to do violent things to people of other faiths and how to work for peace. On one island where they taught, they saw many churches and mosques (Muslim places of worship) that had been burned down. They visited a student of theirs, now a Christian pastor, who had been put in jail. This man had helped save many lives, both Muslim and Christian, when there had been fighting. But because he had criticized some leaders who could have kept the violence from happening, he was put in jail. "Sometimes it is very costly to be a peacemaker," writes Bernie.

On another island where Bernie and Farsijana led a workshop, they visited a village where Christians and Muslims are living in peace with each other. Two years earlier violence between Christians and Muslims had broken out in villages all around this village. Many people were killed and many others fled from the island to find safety. But in this village, where a Christian organization had done much to make people's lives better, not one person was hurt. If angry people came to this village searching for either Christians or Muslims to kill, all the villagers, Muslim and Christian, fled into the jungles together to wait until the killers were gone. God's love at work among these people made a difference. They live with a vision of peace.

Did You Know?

Indonesia is the world's largest archipelago (this means it is a group of islands). It has more than 13,000 islands, but people live on only 6,000 of them.

Prayer

Dear God, be today with refugees in every place. Help children and elderly refugees to stay strong and be hopeful. Help them to see that a new and safer life is possible. Be with the church everywhere as it helps refugees to make homes in new countries. Amen.

Orphans from the conflict in one of the islands of Indonesia learn hand motions for a song.

Word of the Week Vision

Vision means being able to see. It also means being able to look into the future and see something better.

What You Can Do

Having a vision means that no matter how things are right now, you can see in your mind how things could be different. Think of a situation that you find uncomfortable. Maybe you know someone at school or in your neighborhood that people treat badly. Now imagine this person surrounded by people treating that person in a kind way. Let yourself see the person smiling and enjoying the company of others. Is there something you can do to help that vision happen?

Scripture

I wait for the LORD, my soul waits, and in God's word I hope (Psalm 130:5).

MISSION IN THE UNITED STATES

Presbytery of Sierra Blanca

New Mexico

What is your favorite thing to do? Do you like to play the drums? Sew? Skateboard? Maybe one of the things you really like to do is also something you are good at doing. And maybe this is one of the talents or gifts God has given to you.

Adan Soliz (left) leads singing with enthusiasm during worship.

Adan Soliz is a young man who had a gift but didn't know at first how he might use it to share the good news of Jesus Christ. Adan is a talented musician who can play the keyboard and the guitar, sing, and write music. For a while he played in clubs, but then he decided to use his music for God. In summer he plays for religious services that are held in the city parks of Roswell, New Mexico, and during the year he plays and sings at Iglesia Hispana Presbiteriana, where he is a lay pastor. (See the Did You Know? on page 46 to learn what a lay pastor is.) Through his music and ministry Adan especially reaches out to people with a lot of problems who may not attend church. His work as a lay pastor has led him to work with people in prison. In all of his work, Adan reaches back to his roots in music.

Says Adan, "Music hits their soul, even before the word is proclaimed. I see people's eyes, how they show emotion as they receive that blessing. It lays the foundation for them to receive the Word of God." Find the Presbytery of Sierra Blanca on the map on page 112.

Word of the Week

Bible

The Bible is God's Word to us. It is made up of the Hebrew Scriptures, which we call the Old Testament, and the New Testament.

Puzzle: Scrambled Countries

The PC(USA) works in partnership with churches and organizations in these countries of Europe. Eight of the countries have had their names scrambled. Unscramble the names of the eight countries, then see if you can find all the countries on your atlas, globe, or the world map on pages 110–111 in this book.

Albania	Trcaioa
Austria	Czech Republic
Dnnlfai	Rcefan
Georgia	Germany
Greece	Hungary
Leaidrn	Yilta
Lithuania	Netherlands
Poland	Gutprola
Romania	Russia
Slovakia	Slovenia
Pinsa	Nsdeew
Ukraine	Switzerland
Yugoslavia	
United Kingdom	
Belgium	

_____ _____

_____ _____

_____ _____

_____ _____

Answers: Croatia, Finland, France, Ireland, Italy, Portugal, Spain, Sweden

MISSION AROUND THE WORLD

Albania

What happens when the last hymn fades and no one expects the music to ever begin again? What do people do when they close their Bibles knowing they must hide them and never open them to read again? This happened in Albania in 1967 when the government closed all the churches in the country. Across the land, all the Bibles and hymnbooks were gathered up and destroyed. A person found with a Bible was jailed or killed! Yet God's song somehow lived and since 1990 it has been sung again.

For Zefjan Nicolli childhood nights were often spent with the windows tightly closed, curtains pulled, and one candle lit in the center of the room. In the dim light, Zefjan's family gathered and listened to their father quietly recite all the Bible stories he could remember. Zefjan grew up with God's song in his heart although never on his lips. In 1991 when it became legal to practice religion privately, Zefjan heard again about God's redeeming love from a young college mission worker from Seattle, Washington. Zefjan finished his education at the university and became an English interpreter. Today Zefjan helps others hear God's song by providing leadership as the General Secretary for the International Fellowship of Evangelical Students.

When did Presbyterians start giving to the One Great Hour of Sharing offering? The answer is on page 87 in the Mission Yearbook for Prayer & Study.

Prayer

Thank you, God, for giving us your story and the stories of men, women, and children like us in the Bible. Give me wisdom when I read or hear the Bible to listen for the lessons you intend. Give me strength to live in ways that you have shown us are best through the Bible's stories. Amen.

What You Can Do

The Bible has been translated into many languages. There are also many versions or translations of the Bible within the English language. In the *Children's Mission Yearbook,* the New Revised Standard Version of the Bible is used. You may have a *Good News Bible* or a *Jerusalem Bible.* Your grandparents may have grown up reading the King James Bible. Each of these translations tells the stories of the Bible but uses different words to express the meaning. Get your Bible out. What translation is it? Read the Sunday's Gospel reading, John 3:1–17. Now find another Bible from your home or church. See what translation it is and read the same passage. Is one Bible easier for you to understand? Does the meaning change when the words are different?

Giving What You Have

In Albania and many other countries, having a Bible is a luxury. Often families will share a Bible. Do you have a family Bible in your home (one that was handed down to your family from your grandparents)? Put a dollar in your One Great Hour of Sharing coin box for the family Bible in your home. Put 10 cents in the box for every additional Bible in your home.

Did You Know?

The best-selling book in the world is the Bible! It was the very first book ever printed. Johannes Gutenberg printed the first one in 1454. Today the Bible has been translated into 2,018 languages.

MISSION IN THE UNITED STATES
Presbytery of San Fernando
California

How many members do you think your church has? 100? 200? 2,000? The largest Presbyterian church in the United States has 7,962 members! That is larger than some towns! But what would you do if your church had just 30 members? Would you close the doors and tell people to find another church to attend?

Community Presbyterian Church is in Littlerock, California, a small farming community with one stoplight. When the church was started in 1930, it and the town were thriving. But for the past 20 years, the church lost members. It had to decide if it should close its doors or keep going. The Presbytery of San Fernando helped by giving money to Community Presbyterian for redevelopment that allowed the congregation to get a pastor. With new leadership the church slowly began to grow. By 2001 it had 75 members. Another pastor came to the church and programs that reached out to the community were started. These new programs appealed to newcomers in the town, and some members who had quit coming started coming again. A church that once was dying was brought back to life. Find the Presbytery of San Fernando on the map on page 112.

Scripture

Let the hearts of those who seek the LORD rejoice (Psalm 105:3).

Recipe
Porridge

Surprise your family one chilly morning with this favorite Scottish breakfast dish. Ask someone to help when you are using the stove.

Ingredients per person

1 cup of water
1/8 cup of oatmeal
   (don't use instant oatmeal)
1/8 tsp. of salt

Boil the water in a saucepan on the stove. Slowly stir in the oatmeal. Add the salt. Simmer on low heat for 25 minutes. Let stand 3 minutes before serving.

Traditionally, porridge is served in one bowl with a second bowl half filled with cold milk. A person takes a spoonful of porridge and dips it into the milk before it is eaten.

Members of Community Presbyterian Church sing joyfully in worship services.

Word of the Week
Redevelopment

Redevelopment is bringing something, once alive and now dying, back to life. When churches lose a lot of members, sometimes by having new ideas, making changes, and doing some hard work a redevelopment can occur. How have the two churches in the stories on these two pages been redeveloped?

MISSION AROUND THE WORLD

Britain and Ireland

Sometimes when a congregation wants to grow and reach more people with God's good news, it has to . . . give up its church. Westray Parish Kirk (part of the Church of Scotland) is located in Westray, one of the Orkney Isles, which lie off the northern tip of Scotland. If you can, find a map that has Scotland and the Orkney Isles on it. The ferry from Westray takes one and a half hours to reach the main island of the Orkney Isles, and then the mainland of Scotland is still another three hours away by boat. Over the years a lot of people have moved off the island. Only about 600 people live there now.

The church has become much smaller too. The members decided to do something different that would help the whole community. They had their sanctuary, which wasn't in good shape and wasn't used much, made into a community meeting space. Church members have also helped set up a youth center, a playground, and an adult day care. By doing some redevelopment, the church continues to be an important part of the island community.

The island of Westray, off the northern tip of Scotland, is known for its beauty.

Did You Know?

The Orkney island just east of Westray is Papa Westray, where the oldest known house in northern Europe still stands. Someone lived there before the first pyramids were built in Egypt.

Prayer

God of creation and Lord of the church, be with congregations—small ones and big ones. May our congregations respond to the changes around them in ways that keep your story and love present to men and women and boys and girls. Amen.

Giving What You Have

For every chore you do in your household, put 25 cents in the One Great Hour of Sharing coin box.

What languages are spoken in Britain? Find the answer in the Mission Yearbook for Prayer & Study *on the page about Britain/Ireland. Look in the gray box for the answer.*

What You Can Do

Is there a place in your home or yard that needs "redevelopment"? Maybe your closet or chest of drawers is always a mess and needs some new ideas for keeping things in order and in places you can remember. Maybe your whole room needs redevelopment! Think of something in your life that could use some attention and a new way of doing things, then do something!

MISSION IN THE UNITED STATES

Presbytery of Los Ranchos

California

The weather channel said there would be rain, and the way the clouds were hanging over the town of Ladera Ranch, no one doubted that it indeed was going to rain. But, it just couldn't rain on this evening. If the story of Jesus' birth was going to be told, it needed to be a dry evening. It was the first Christmas Eve service of the Village Presbyterian Church, a new church development of the Presbytery of Los Ranchos that did not yet have its own church building. Ever since the pastor had begun services for the community in July, meeting outside had not been a problem. It was southern California after all and the weather had for the most part been very nice. Wanting to leave nothing to chance, the pastor had tried to rent a space in town where the service could be held. Nothing was available. After worrying about not having a place, the pastor and the church people preparing the service decided to go ahead and have an outdoor service. Not having a good indoor place for the service helped the new congregation understand what Mary and Joseph went through when they got to Bethlehem. After all, Jesus was born in a stable because there was no place for him in the inn or anywhere else in Bethlehem.

As the congregation gathered for this first Christmas Eve service, it seemed the rain would pour down at any second. But it didn't. Many people in the community joined the congregation to sing carols and to welcome the baby Jesus. Following the benediction, many stayed to visit and share in the joy of the night. And then, after everything was packed up and people were ready to go home, it happened. The rain came down in buckets! Many blessings were showered down on Village Presbyterian Church that evening, including new members joining the church and the love of God reaching out into the community to welcome others. Find the Presbytery of Los Ranchos on the map on page 112.

VILLAGE PRESBYTERIAN CHURCH

Scripture

I lift up my eyes to the hills—from where will my help come? My help comes from the LORD (Psalm 121:1–2).

The Rev. Steve Wright presides over the first baptism at Village Presbyterian Church.

Recipe

Baked Rice with a Kick

Here's a rice dish with a Tex-Mex taste. It's delicious!

Ingredients

1 cup quick-cook brown rice
2 cups sour cream
1 cup shredded cheddar cheese
8-oz. can green chilies
1/2 stick of butter
1/4 cup Parmesan cheese

Cook the quick-cook rice so you have one full cup. Combine rice and sour cream. Grease a casserole dish and spread half the rice mixture on the bottom. Sprinkle half the shredded cheese over the rice. Drain the can of green chilies and spread chilies over the shredded cheese. Sprinkle remaining shredded cheese over the chilies. The other half of the rice should be spread over all this. Cut up and put pieces of the butter on top and then sprinkle all over with Parmesan cheese. Bake in a preheated 350-degree oven for 35 minutes.

MISSION AROUND THE WORLD

Iraq

Iraq is a country that has been in the news for some time now. Find it on the world map on page 111 and find where your home state is so you can see how far away Iraq is. A man from Kentucky has been serving in the U.S. Army in Baghdad, Iraq, but his job is different from the soldiers. He is a chaplain, which means he's a minister who works with the soldiers. Chaplain Brenson Bishop happens also to be Presbyterian. It has been very dangerous where Chaplain Bishop is working, so he does all he can to give support to the soldiers. He listens to them when they need to talk and gives them words of encouragement. He prays with them, reads Scripture to them, and offers them his friendship. Sometimes it is very difficult for him, but his faith in God keeps him going and gives him what he needs to help the men and women in his care.

Chaplain Bishop knows that the young men and women, who are mostly between the ages of 18 and 26, face the possibility of being killed every day as they try to keep more fighting from happening. Sometimes they have to fight, and some of them have had to kill people. Such experiences change them. Chaplain Bishop comforts them and helps them see that God is present with them even in such a hard place when they are doing hard things. Chaplain Bishop is one of about 355 chaplains of the Presbyterian Council for Chaplains and Military Personnel who serve in the U.S. military forces.

Prayer

Dear God, we pray for people in Iraq whose lives are so hard now. We pray for the soldiers who are there. We pray that the fighting may end and your peace may come to Iraq. We ask that you give strength and courage to the chaplains who try to show everyone that God is present even in the hardest times. In Jesus' name. Amen.

Did You Know?

Presbyterian chaplains have been working with U.S. soldiers since the American Revolution and have served soldiers in every war the United States has fought. But there wasn't an organization of Presbyterian chaplains until 1973, when the Presbyterian Council for Chaplains and Military Personnel was formed.

Giving What You Have

Part of the money received from the One Great Hour of Sharing goes to projects of the Presbyterian Disaster Assistance. One of these projects is repairing the water systems in cities near Baghdad, Iraq. Put 10 cents in your offering coin box for every water faucet you have in your house.

What You Can Do

You can help chaplains in the army by letting soldiers who are living overseas know that you care about them and reminding them that God cares about them also. Write a letter or e-mail to a soldier. If you don't know of a soldier in your congregation, ask your pastor if he or she knows of one in your presbytery.

Word of the Week Chaplain

A chaplain is a minister who works with an organization other than a church. Some chaplains work in hospitals, some in the military forces like Chaplain Bishop, and others in colleges and other places.

MISSION IN THE UNITED STATES

Presbytery of Santa Barbara

California

Have you ever experienced the joy of swinging in a big swing on a big front porch, sipping a cool drink, listening to the ceiling fans whirl above you? Large front porches give us a feeling of welcome and invite us to "come sit and chat a spell." When the Presbyterian campus ministry at the University of California at Santa Barbara began plans to expand its ministry and reach more students, the planners wanted to bring back those images of sitting on the front porch.

The Front PORCH ministry was developed to give college students a chance to come together to worship, grow in their thinking as Christians, discuss with others questions about their faith, and see the good news in a new way. (PORCH stands for Presbyterians of Reasoned Christian Hope.) At

Scripture

But how are they to call on one in whom they have not believed? And how are they to believe in one of whom they have never heard? And how are they to hear without someone to proclaim him? And how are they to proclaim him unless they are sent? As it is written, "How beautiful are the feet of those who bring good news!". . . So faith comes from what is heard, and what is heard comes through the word of Christ (Romans 10:14–15, 17).

the Front PORCH all students are welcome and can find a home away from home. At a time when students are faced with new ideas and values, the Front PORCH can help them learn and grow as Christians, just as they are learning and growing in other ways. The Front PORCH has been so successful at the university in Santa Barbara that the idea is starting to spread to other campuses. It's in the Presbytery of Santa Barbara, which you can find on the map on page 112.

Word Puzzle: Crossing through the Words

Cross through words describing weather, names of two men who preached, words that describe parts of a house, and the word that means followers of Jesus. Beginning at the top left, read the words that remain to find the message.

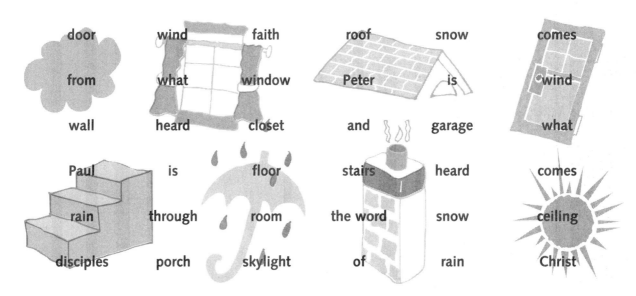

door   wind   faith   roof   snow   comes

from   what   window   Peter   is   wind

wall   heard   closet   and   garage   what

Paul   is   floor   stairs   heard   comes

rain   through   room   the word   snow   ceiling

disciples   porch   skylight   of   rain   Christ

MISSION AROUND THE WORLD

Lithuania

*Let your children follow only the paths of virtue,
working for the good of their native land and for
all mankind.
Let the sun banish all darkness from Lithuania,
with light and truth always guiding our steps.*

This verse from the Lithuanian national anthem is proudly sung each day at schools and at public ceremonies. It is sung with a great deal of emotion and love of country. This is because for 700 years Lithuania was a country under someone else's rule. It did not have its own national anthem. Only since 1991 have Lithuanians had their own anthem to sing with joy and respect.

In the 14 years that Lithuania has been independent, its people have worked hard to establish a strong new government. This period of adjustment has given the Evangelical Reformed Church of Lithuania reason to sing, as it has sought to let the light and truth of the gospel shine. More and more young people are hearing the call to follow Christ and are answering the need for more church leaders by going to school to learn about being ministers. These young people who are committed to sharing the good news are growing and bringing energy to the Reformed congregations in the country, many whose roots date back to the sixteenth century. Find Lithuania on the map on pages 110–111.

Young people share the good news in Lithuania.

Prayer

Dear God, be welcome in my heart and life. May I always welcome you and your love into my life and show it in my actions. Amen.

Did You Know?

Lithuania's national anthem was originally a hymn written in 1898. In 1918, twenty years after the hymn was written, Lithuania was finally declared an independent state after 700 years of living under other countries' rule. Then in 1940 it became part of Russia. It took Lithuanians another 53 years to achieve total independence and democracy.

Giving What You Have

This week put a dollar in your One Great Hour of Sharing coin box if you have a front porch and another dollar if you have a back porch or deck.

Word of the Week

Good news

The good news is the message of God's amazing love and grace to each of us shown in the life, death, and resurrection of Jesus Christ.

What You Can Do

Think about a particular way you are aware that God loves you. Ask a couple of people, like a parent, friend, or church school teacher, if they have a particular story that reminds them of God's love for them. Share with them the way you are aware of God's love. Sometimes it feels awkward to share the good news of God's love with others. But sharing our faith through our words, stories, and actions is an important part of being a follower of Jesus Christ.

Scripture

Your hands have made and fashioned me; give me understanding that I may learn your commandments. Those who fear you shall see me and rejoice, because I have hoped in your word (Psalm 119:73–74).

MISSION IN THE UNITED STATES

Peace River Presbytery

Florida

Some time this week when you are eating a meal, look down at your plate. If there is a fruit or vegetable somewhere on it, ask the person who shops in your home if the fruit or vegetable came from the United States. If it did, it is likely that a migrant farm worker originally picked it. Migrant farm workers are people who move around the country following the growing seasons of farms. Migrant workers do not get paid much. They usually live in run-down housing provided for them by the farmers. The children of migrant workers must begin at a new school each new season, or they have to work alongside their parents in the fields. There is no child care for young children, so they go into the fields with their parents or are left alone.

The people in Peace River Presbytery and the Presbytery of Tampa Bay decided to do something about the migrant workers. These two presbyteries formed the Beth-El Farm Worker Ministry, which offers migrant workers and their families everything from worship, Bible study, and summer camp to a child-care nursery, a soccer league, a preschool, and a school in which both English and Spanish are spoken. Beth-El is also working on a place where sick migrant workers can stay until they are well. The members of the churches in both the Tampa Bay and Peace River Presbyteries have shown compassion to migrant workers. Find these two presbyteries on the map on page 112.

Craft
Holy Week Table Tent

This week is called Holy Week, also called Passion Week. Holy Week celebrates the last week of Jesus' life on earth, starting with Palm Sunday and ending with Easter. Make a Holy Week Table Tent that will help you remember the events of this week. You may want to place it on your table and use it at meal times.

Materials
11 x 17" copy paper
stapler
crayons or markers
scissors
hole punch
tea light candle

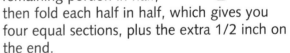

Fold the paper in half, creating two long horizontal rectangles, and cut along the fold. (You will need one half page for each table tent.) Fold over 1/2 inch on one short end of the paper. Fold the remaining portion in half, then fold each half in half, which gives you four equal sections, plus the extra 1/2 inch on the end.

Color each of the four sections with images that relate to the events of Holy Week: a palm branch for Palm Sunday; a cup and bread for the Last Supper; a pitcher of water and towel for when Jesus washed the disciples' feet; and three crosses for the crucifixion. Staple the 1/2-inch tab to the other end of the paper on the inside, creating an open box shape. Punch holes in the paper to allow light to shine through. Place a candle in the center and light it at mealtimes. Make sure an adult is present.

Option: You can copy the prayer for this week on your Table Tent and use it as a table blessing.

MISSION AROUND THE WORLD

Croatia

People who have a disability or are sick have needs besides physical ones. In one class that PC(USA) mission co-worker Brett McMichael teaches at the Evangelical Theological College in Osijek, Croatia, students learn how to care for them in other ways. Brett has students pair off. One person pretends to be a caregiver, the other person pretends to have a disability that leaves him or her blind, deaf, or unable to move in some way. The pairs then do the things students at the college normally do—go to the library, eat a meal, walk down hallways and up and down stairs, play sports, attend classes—all the time in their roles as caregiver and person with a disability. Quickly students learn the challenges of everyday activities without sight, hearing, or abilities to walk or use hands. They also realize how much work and energy a caregiver gives to help a person with disabilities. "I found being without the use of my legs difficult—but I expected that to be the case," said one student. "What I was not so prepared for was how demanding it can be to be a caregiver." These future Christian leaders from Croatia are learning to have compassion, and will be good examples of caring in their churches and communities. Find Croatia on the map on page 110–111.

Brett is a mission worker who helps people learn about living with disabilities.

Word of the Week Compassion

When we have compassion we feel for and care about someone and have the desire to help that person.

Prayer

God, bless the migrant workers everywhere who help to bring us good food. Help our leaders find the ways to make their lives better. Give hope to all those who have lost legs or arms or sight or hearing, and give compassion to those who work with them. In Jesus' name. Amen.

What You Can Do

The Presbyterian Disaster Assistance program supports a worldwide group of churches that have responded to the need for land-mine removal in many countries where land mines were "planted" during civil wars. Women and children are often injured by these mines as they work in the fields or walk to school. Land mines have killed thousands, but even more people have been left without sight, hearing, or limbs. Find out how you, your family, and your church can support efforts to remove land mines by logging onto www.pcusa.org/pda and going to Resources and Mission Tools.

Did You Know?

Land mines cost less than $5 to make and "plant" but about $1,000 dollars to remove! They can be dangerous for as long as twenty years. Part of the money collected from the One Great Hour of Sharing Offering goes to Presbyterian Disaster Assistance, which sends money to help remove land mines.

Giving What You Have

For each fruit and vegetable you eat this week put 10 cents in your One Great Hour of Sharing coin box. For every pair of glasses (including sunglasses) and every set of headphones you own to listen to music or your computer, give 50 cents.

One Great Hour of Sharing

MISSION IN THE UNITED STATES

Presbytery of South Louisiana

The land of southern Louisiana is very low, so when there's a big storm, it tends to flood. In 2002, two hurricanes, Isadora and Lili, hit the area within a few weeks. The people of the area usually stick together and help each other out, but there was more damage than they could handle. So people at the First Presbyterian Church in Thibodaux (TIB-oh-doh), a member church of the Presbytery of South Louisiana, began looking for more ways to help. The Rev. Bill Crawford recalls, "We're not that great with hammers and saws, so we'd likely be in the way down there. Our folks kept asking, 'What do we have to offer?' until we came up with an answer. We got the idea to host the groups that come down to work with the people affected by the disasters. We put up the money for a building with showers and bathrooms next to the church, and some groups came down to help us do the building itself. Pretty soon, we were able to welcome groups from Nebraska and Virginia that came down to help with rebuilding the areas damaged by the hurricanes. In this case, the strangers the church was welcoming were people who came to help the community get back on its feet."

Find the Presbytery of South Louisiana on the map on page 112.

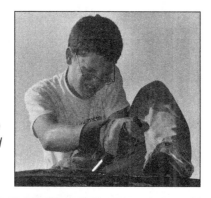

Thanks to First Presbyterian in Thibodaux, people like this worker who came to help rebuild homes had a place to stay.

Scripture

"When was it that we saw you a stranger and welcomed you, or naked and gave you clothing?" (Matthew 25:38).

What You Can Do

Make a point every day this week to notice one person who may be feeling left out. Think of one thing you can do that will help that person feel more comfortable and welcome.

Word of the Week
Welcome

This word is usually an automatic answer when someone says "thank you." But it means so much more. At its root, it means "You are well come," or "We're so glad you're here." Making someone feel welcome is at the center of what Jesus asks us to do. In this week's passage, Jesus tells us that it's important to make people welcome even when it isn't easy.

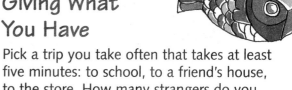

Giving What You Have

Pick a trip you take often that takes at least five minutes: to school, to a friend's house, to the store. How many strangers do you see just in that short time? Since you can't welcome all of them personally, put 5 cents for each one in your One Great Hour of Sharing offering bank.

One
great hour of sharing

MISSION AROUND THE WORLD

Bosnia and Herzegovina

In the 1990s a terrible war between different ethnic and religious groups destroyed the lives of many communities in Bosnia and Herzegovina, a country in southern Europe. Many families could not have survived without aid from One Great Hour of Sharing, which is distributed through Church World Service, a mission partnership of many churches, including the PC(USA). Grateful for that aid, the communities set up an unusual "payback" process to help other hungry people in their land. That process asks that those who received aid contribute a part of their crops to support others in need, especially people of different ethnic groups. Their gift of fresh potatoes—twelve tons of them!—was very welcome in seven soup kitchens around the country.

Families from both sides of the war have contributed to the potato harvest, and their food is given to people based on need, not on ethnic background. Hika Sator, one of the men loading a truck of potatoes, said, "The only important thing to me is that the person eating these potatoes is hungry." Another farmer said, "Now I'm back on my land, and I know there are people who care about us, who pray for us, and who support us." By reaching out to help others, these families are helping to build peace in a country still troubled by the memories of war.

Did You Know?

Almost half (49 percent) of the population of Bosnia and Herzegovina have a standard of living below or close to the poverty line.

Prayer

Dear God, we want to do as Jesus did and told us to do: to welcome the strangers among us. Let your love shine out through us and help us to share it by making those we may not know very well know that they are welcome, and let our lives enrich each other. In the love of your son Jesus. Amen.

Recipe

Pine Nut Sweet Bread

One of the most traditional ways of welcoming people is to share your food with them. Bread is a common food to share, since almost all peoples have some kind of bread as a part of their diet. This pine nut sweet bread made from squash or pumpkins comes from the southwestern region of the United States. It goes well with soups or stews and can also work as a dessert, especially if you serve ice cream or yogurt over it.

Preheat the oven to 350 degrees.
In a mixing bowl, combine:
1 1/2 cup unbleached flour
1/2 tsp. salt
1 tsp. baking powder
3/4 cup brown sugar
1 tsp. cinnamon
1 tsp. grated nutmeg

Stir in:
1 cup of finely mashed or pureed pumpkin or squash
2 eggs beaten foamy
1/2 cup melted butter

Stir 3/4 cup pine nuts into this thick batter and scrape it into a greased 6 x 9" loaf pan. Bake for one hour or until a knife inserted in the bread comes out clean.

MISSION IN THE UNITED STATES

Cherokee Presbytery

Georgia

More than three years ago the people of Ray-Thomas Memorial Presbyterian Church in Marietta started praying together to find ways their church could do mission with people from other countries who had moved into their community. When a group of Presbyterians from Brazil came looking for a place to meet, the church realized this was their opportunity. The Ray-Thomas congregation invited the group from Brazil to use their church building to hold services on Sunday evenings. Both congregations wanted more, but they did not know what they could do since they had different languages and ways of doing things. Eating together is a good way to get to know others better, so each congregation hosted a dinner for

Scripture

By God's great mercy God has given us a new birth into a living hope through the resurrection of Jesus Christ from the dead (I Peter 1:3).

the other congregation. After the dinners both congregations decided to worship together. They held a service where both English and Portuguese were spoken and leaders from both congregations took part.

The Rev. Carrie Scott, Ray-Thomas's pastor, is happy about how the two congregations have helped each other. "We have taught the Brazilians about budgets, and they have taught us anew about the excitement of the gospel." The goal for these two congregations is now to become one church with leadership from both. Find Cherokee Presbytery, where the two congregations are located, on the map on page 112.

Puzzle

Coming Together Maze

Help the members of Ray-Thomas Memorial Presbyterian Church and the group from Brazil as they start on their own paths and then join together to become one church.

RAY-THOMAS MEMORIAL PRESBYTERIAN CHURCH

PRESBYTERIANS FROM BRAZIL

ONE CHURCH

Giving What You Have

Find out how many years your church has been in existence. For each year put 5 cents in the offering plate this Sunday.

Did You Know?

People who want to be ministers often go to special schools to learn how to be ministers. They are called seminaries. Sometimes they are called schools of theology, like the Near East School of Theology. (Look at the Word of the Week on page 95 to find out what theology means.) The PC(USA) supports 11 seminaries.

What You Can Do

In Cherokee Presbytery, two congregations hosted dinners for each other. After the dinners they decided to worship together. Eating *is* a good way for people to get to know each other. Is there a new family in your church or in your neighborhood? Ask your parents or caregivers to help you plan and fix a meal for a new family. Invite the family over to share the meal you fix.

Word of the Week Resurrection

Resurrection is the rising to life from death. We celebrated the resurrection of Jesus last week in our Easter services. It can also mean a renewal. Churches and programs can be resurrected, or given new life, by following God's leading to reach new people with the message of God's good news.

Prayer

God, thank you for ministers everywhere who lead our churches and teach us about you. Bless them and bless the people who are now studying in schools to become ministers. In Jesus' name. Amen.

Do you know which PC(USA)-related seminary is nearest to where you live? Find out where the seminaries are on page 370 in the Mission Yearbook for Prayer & Study.

MISSION AROUND THE WORLD

Lebanon

Several years ago Mary Mikhael was living in Lebanon attending the Near East School of Theology (NEST) when she learned she could go to the United States and study Christian education at the Presbyterian School of Christian Education in Richmond, Virginia. Mary couldn't wait to go. During her two years in Richmond Mary learned a lot about the church, the Bible, and the United States. As she prepared to return home to Lebanon to teach, the news came that Israel had invaded Lebanon. She was unable to go home. The PC(USA) and NEST decided to help Mary get more schooling in the United States, and so she studied at Columbia University and at Union Theological Seminary in New York City. When her studies were complete, things were better in Lebanon, and Mary was able to return home. Today Mary serves as president of NEST, which teaches Christians from all over the Middle East and North Africa. Find Lebanon on the map on pages 110–111.

Dr. Mary Mikhael is president of the Near East School of Theology in Beirut, Lebanon.

MISSION IN THE UNITED STATES

St. Augustine Presbytery

Florida

What does baseball have to do with church? Riverside Presbyterian Church in Jacksonville is teaching us! The Return Baseball to the Inner City (RBI) program reaches out to children and youth both in the church and outside the church in the community. Many of the young players who are involved in this program come from a nearby homeless shelter; others come from a neighborhood without many resources. RBI gives the players not only the chance to play baseball but also to make new friends from different backgrounds. The Riverside Church brings a spiritual element to the program, which allows the young people to see how God can be present in all their activities.

"Here batter, batter, batter, batter swing!" may sound like an unusual call to worship. But each season as the number of participants grows, so do the stories of how God is moving in young people's lives through RBI. Riverside Presbyterian Church is in St. Augustine Presbytery. Find this presbytery on the map on page 112.

Volunteers help out in other after-school programs at Riverside Presbyterian Church.

Scripture

Jesus unrolled the scroll and found the place where it was written: The Spirit of the Lord is upon me, because he has anointed me to bring good news to the poor (Luke 4:17b–18a).

Craft

Red-Figure or Black-Figure Pot Painting

Before 530 BC the people in Greece painted in what is now called black figure. This means they painted human and animal figures with black paint on a red background. After 530 BC the people in Greece began painting in red figure. This means they painted their figures red and the background was black.

Try your hand at creating a red-figure or black-figure pot like the ancient Greeks!

Materials

1 medium-size terra-cotta pot
3 paint brushes of varying sizes
1 container of black tempera paint
1 container of red tempera paint
2 throwaway containers (like small
   plastic cups)
newspaper
pencil

Cover your work surface with newspaper. Put some black paint in one container and red paint in the other container. Decide whether you will be doing red-figure or black-figure painting. With the pencil lightly draw an outline of a human, animal, or plant on the pot. Use the red or black paint (depending  on which type of painting you are doing) to fill in your figure. Let it dry. Then paint the background with the opposite color.

Giving What You Have

The Pentecost Offering (see pages 44–45) is coming up May 15. Get an offering coin box from your church if you can. For every sport you play throughout the year, save 25 cents for the Pentecost Offering.

Word of the Week
Evangelism

Evangelism comes from the Greek word evangel, which means "good news." Evangelism is sharing the good news of God's love in Christ.

What You Can Do

Think about the many ways God's word is spread through the world. Look at the stories on these two pages to help you think of ways. What is a way you can share the good news with people near to you?

Did You Know?

The Greeks invented sports contests around 700 BC. These contests and festivals were held to honor the Greek gods. The most famous of the games were held in a town called Olympia. (That's where we take the name and the idea for our current Olympic games.) The early games took place every four years. Foot races, wrestling, boxing, javelin hurling, discus throwing, and horseracing were all part of the contests.

Prayer

Dear God, whether we are playing baseball or sitting in a church service, whether we are telling others about you or helping a friend with homework, we can let others know the good news of your love—just by the way we do these things and everything else. Thank you for your love and for sending Jesus to show us how to live. Amen.

MISSION AROUND THE WORLD

Greece

Does evangelism sound like something only a few people can do? Spreading the good news of God's love—doing evangelism—can be done in many ways. The Greek Evangelical Church, a partner of the PC(USA), has been spreading the good news in a neighboring country, Albania. Look on the map on pages 110–111 and find Greece and Albania. A few years ago the pastor of the Greek Evangelical Church in Corfu, Greece, made friends with a young Albanian living in Greece and taught him about being a follower of Christ. That young man is now the pastor of a mission church in Albania that was started by visiting Greek Christians telling Albanians about Christ. The mission church has grown and is telling others about God in many ways: by giving food and clothing to people in need, by helping refugees, and by showing others in the way they live what being a follower of Christ means.

When one of the leaders of the Greek Church was visiting the Albanian mission church, an Albanian woman asked him to pray with her to accept Christ in her heart. He writes: "'Why do you want to become a Christian?' This lady responded, 'For two years now I have been watching the change Christ made in the life of my husband's brother who became a believer because he was watching the change in his wife's life, and now I want to become like them. I hope I can be a good example to my husband.' A year later her husband became a Christian as well. Today both are leading a new church endeavor in their village."

MISSION IN THE UNITED STATES

Yellowstone Presbytery

Montana

Is that chicken and dumplings I smell cooking? Smells like a "Wonderful Wednesday" to me! The delicious smells coming from the Manhattan Presbyterian Church kitchen are only a part of what make Wednesday "wonderful" in this small community. At least 40 elementary-school-aged children come each week with their families for worship, Bible study, crafts, games, and a home-cooked meal. "We like to call ourselves 'the little church with the big God,'" says the Rev. Debbie Funke. Worship and Bible study are important elements in Wonderful Wednesday, but what

Scripture

The LORD is my shepherd, I shall not want. He makes me lie down in green pastures; he leads me beside still waters; he restores my soul (Psalm 23:1–3).

many who attend like best are the fellowship and conversation about faith that occur around the table during the meal. For many of these families, this is the only meal they will eat together during the week. The church also sends some of these neighborhood children to summer camp each year, where they have time to do Bible study and play in a beautiful setting.

Manhattan Church is in the town of Manhattan, Montana, and is part of Yellowstone Presbytery. Find this presbytery on the map on page 112.

Puzzle

Counting Sheep

Add the sum of the values of the letters in "The Lord is my shepherd" to find out how many sheep are in the shepherd's flock. Now divide the sum by 100 and round to the nearest whole number to find today's psalm. It really works!

1	2	3	4	5	6	7	8	9	10	11	12	13	14	15	16	17	18	19	20	21	22	23	24	25	26
A	B	C	D	E	F	G	H	I	J	K	L	M	N	O	P	Q	R	S	T	U	V	W	X	Y	Z

Suzanne Bratsky

Children from Manhattan, Montana, enjoy summer camp.

MISSION AROUND THE WORLD

Iran

The city of Bam, in southwestern Iran, is surprisingly green to be in the middle of the desert. Palm and date trees surround this busy city, and many farmers have date and citrus farms. Others keep herds of sheep and goats that eat the grass and other greenery. On December 26, 2003, an earthquake devastated Bam, leaving 27,000 people dead and 60,000 people homeless. Sixty percent of the buildings in the city were destroyed, and the old part of the city that had stood for over 2,000 years was severely damaged and in some areas completely flattened. Many of the farms surrounding the city were also destroyed. The world community, including the PC(USA), responded immediately. Presbyterian Disaster Assistance committed $150,000 in emergency relief aid to help survivors. Money from One Great Hour of Sharing (see pages 30–31) helped purchase emergency shelter supplies and water tanks for survivors.

Two PC(USA) partners, Action by Churches Together and the Middle East Council of Churches, continue to support work that will repair damage to the city and will help farmers who have lost their homes, animals, and crops. Presbyterian Disaster Assistance funds continue to go to Bam to improve water systems. Hygiene kits, blankets, and tents are also being sent to Bam from Church World Service. The tragedy in Bam shows how the church around the world can work together to respond to the needs of all God's people.

Prayer

Look through your church directory or think about the people in your congregation. Pray for them—pray for their healing, for strength for older adults, for guidance for the young. Pray for the fellowship and friendship among members of your congregation and within the neighborhood.

What You Can Do

Earth Day falls within this week. Decide on ways you can help the environment by polluting less. Walk or ride your bike when you can instead of asking someone to drive you. See if there are times you can use public transportation. Encourage your family to think about ways you can cut back on adding more chemicals into the environment in your neighborhood.

Word of the Week Fellowship

A fellowship is a gathering of people who are friends or who are of a common mind. In the church we are a fellowship of believers.

Did You Know?

Sheep were among the first animals to be domesticated, beginning more than 6,000 years ago! There are now more than 800 breeds of domestic sheep in the world. In Iran there are 27 kinds of sheep.

Giving What You Have

Call on one or two older church members and ask them to tell you about what the church they grew up in was like. They will probably enjoy your interest and your visit, and you will learn a lot about how the church both changes and stays the same.

MISSION IN THE UNITED STATES

Presbytery of Western Colorado

Cautiously, the family entered the sanctuary and found seats on the back pew. The first hymn had just begun. Nine-year-old Lane Chabarria had been invited to come to worship on this morning by his older friend, Robert Harrington. Lane had asked his family to come with him. Although they were not churchgoers, Lane's mother, stepfather, grandmother, and younger brother agreed to go with him. Lane and his brother joined the other children at the front of the sanctuary during the children's sermon. Next to him Lane could see the covered Communion table. He wondered what it was and why it was in the church. "What is under the white sheet?" Lane asked the minister. The minister said, "Let's take a look." Then he lifted the cloth to show the Communion elements. "Look at all the tiny glasses!" exclaimed Lane. The minister then explained the Lord's Supper and the amazing way that Jesus loves us. Lane was very excited. He had never been to church before but now he definitely wanted to come back.

The church Lane and his family were invited to is in a rural community and is one of the smallest churches in the Presbytery of Western Colorado. (Can you find this presbytery on the map on page 112?) The church had only 50 members when it decided to try out new ways to bring people into church. With prayer, support from the presbytery, and a new full-time minister, this church has opened its doors and hearts to its diverse community and is reaching out to people like Lane and his family. Now Native Americans, Anglo Americans, Hispanics, ranchers, professionals, retirees, children, youth, and adults all have found a home where they can share their love of Jesus Christ.

Word of the Week   Litany

A litany is an order of worship or a prayer with repeated responses to be said by God's people.

Scripture

Do not be conformed to this world, but be transformed by the renewing of your minds, so that you may discern what is the will of God—what is good and acceptable and perfect (Romans 12:2).

Recipe

Communion Bread

In 1/2 cup warm water mix 1 tbs. honey and 1 package dry active yeast. In a separate saucepan heat 3 cups milk to just before it boils, and then add 1/4 lb. butter, 2 tsp. salt, 1/4 cup honey, and 1/2 cup wheat germ. Let this milk mixture cool for 15 minutes and then add 1 cup white flour and 1 cup whole wheat flour. Stir this milk mixture together with the yeast mixture and let it sit for 1 hour.

After 1 hour add 3 1/2 cups whole wheat flour and 3 1/2 cups white flour to the mixture. Stir vigorously with a wooden spoon. Knead dough into a ball. Place in a warm spot and let rise to twice its size. Turn out onto a floured board and knead again. Add more flour if dough is sticky. Put dough in a bowl that has been buttered and floured, cover with a towel, and place in a warm spot to rise again—about 1 hour or until it has risen twice its size.

Cut dough into 1 dozen loaves, cut slits in the tops, and place on a greased baking sheet. Bake at 400 degrees for 15 minutes, then lower the temperature to 325 degrees and bake for another 15 or 20 minutes. Each loaf will serve between 30 and 50 people for Communion. You can seal the loaves in plastic wrap or bags and freeze.

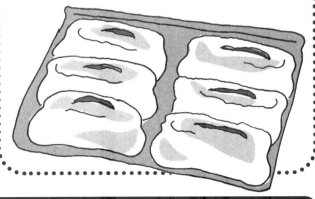

MISSION AROUND THE WORLD

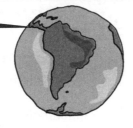

Nicaragua

*The sun and the green coffee fields
melt together on the horizon
and in the thickness the cenzontle bird sings;
life comes back to the corral
and I feel the fragrant air,
a mixture of sweat and good smells,
and you ask me to sing,
and I sing to you, my Lord.*

This verse from a popular song in Nicaragua paints a picture in our minds of nature and enjoying God's creation. (Find this country on the map on page 110.) Although Nicaragua has been a country torn apart by fighting, the worship life of its people is full of songs of praise and thanksgiving as well as songs urging Christians to take action for justice.

The chorus of another song is like a litany. It reminds the people of Nicaragua that they are not alone. It is a good reminder for God's people throughout the world.

*The Lord is close, the Lord is close.
Close to my people, close to the one who struggles out of love.
The Lord is close, the Lord is close.
The Lord is the pilgrim who shares my pain.*

Giving What You Have

For every coffee cup or mug in your house, put 5 cents in your Pentecost Offering coin box.

North Americans and Nicaraguans sing together during a 2004 visit by North Americans to Nicaragua.

Did You Know?

Coffee is one of the major crops grown in Nicaragua. The Presbyterian Coffee Project works with Equal Exchange, a project that helps poor coffee farmers with small farms in Africa, Asia, and Central America—including Nicaragua—make a fair profit from selling coffee. Sometimes coffee prices drop so low that the small farms and farm workers cannot make enough money for basic human needs. Equal Exchange trades with the small farmers so that they can make enough money to live. When Presbyterians buy coffee through the Presbyterian Coffee Project, they help support these farmers.

What You Can Do

Find out from someone in your church's office or the person in charge of the worship committee when your church will next celebrate Communion. Offer to have your family bake bread for use that week. (You can bake bread and freeze it for use within three months' time). Then, using the recipe on page 38 or one of your favorite bread recipes, bake bread for your family and for the church. You may even want to bring a loaf to a new member or a favorite church school teacher.

Prayer

Sometimes we stir our food—to stir in sugar, to cool a hot drink, or to mix fruit into cereal. As you stir your soup, hot chocolate, or cereal, ask God's blessing for the day and guidance for your life. See if you can stir and pray in rhythm. *Thank you, God, for this new day . . . Go with me, God, throughout the day.*

Scripture

Whenever you face trials of any kind, consider it nothing but joy, because you know that the testing of your faith produces endurance; and let endurance have its full effect, so that you may be mature and complete, lacking in nothing (James 1:2–4).

MISSION IN THE UNITED STATES

Presbytery of Wyoming

Chairs and tables for desks filled the room. The room looked like a classroom but it used to be something very different—a home for chickens! Mrs. Vida Dzobo, a retired teacher, turned an old chicken coop into a classroom for a new high school in the town of Ho, Ghana, because of a shortage of secondary schools (grades 10–12). Only about 60 percent of children in Ghana ever go to school. Those who do attend school often drop out by the sixth grade because their families can't afford to send them anymore, or because there is no school nearby. Yet, only a good education will qualify a young person, especially a girl, for one of the few, well-paying jobs in Ghana. With lots of faith and endurance but very little money, Mrs. Dzobo began her school.

The Presbytery of Wyoming learned about Mrs. Dzobo's work and the students' needs after a representative from the presbytery, Sherry Flyr, flew to Ghana with some other Presbyterians from the United States and met Mrs. Dzobo. They made the trip through what is called a Global Exchange, sponsored by Presbyterian Women. After Sherry Flyr came home, she spent two years telling Mrs. Dzobo's story throughout the presbytery and the Synod of the Rocky Mountains. Enough money has now been raised to construct a new building with four classrooms as well as to start work on a three-story building for education and community gatherings. Chickens are still abundant in Ho, but now they don't share their coops with teenagers interested in learning! Find the Presbytery of Wyoming on the map on page 112.

Craft
Fun-shaped Book

Make a book from the heart. Heart-shaped or other fun-shaped books can be used to let grandparents know they are special or to keep a journal of your thoughts and prayers.

Materials

1 or 2 pieces of heavy paper or tagboard
sheets of white paper
scissors
hole punch
ribbon
crayons, markers, or other materials
  to decorate with

Decide on a shape: heart, leaf, flag, sun, or something else. Choose a piece of heavy paper or tagboard. You can even use old file folders. Fold in half and draw the shape on the front. Cut out the shape. This will give you the front and back covers of the book. Then trace the shape onto the top sheet of a few pages of white paper and cut out. You should be able to cut several sheets of white paper at once. Holding the front and back covers together as one shape, use a hole punch to make one or two holes in the left side of the covers. Then place the white paper between the two covers and punch holes in the white paper also, using the holes in the covers as your guide. Use ribbon to tie the book together. Decorate the cover.

Make a mini version of this book and use it as a birthday greeting or a special note to someone.

Students and teachers at Dora Memorial School Complex in Ho, Ghana, are constructing the new secondary school building.

MISSION AROUND THE WORLD

Honduras

If you had to search for even an ounce of fresh water, beg for the tiniest piece of fresh fruit, or walk no matter how far away you had to travel, would your songs be joyful? Though most of the people in Honduras are poor and their lives full of daily struggles just to survive and endure hard times, their songs are not all about their suffering. Gloria and Tim Wheeler, PC(USA) partners in mission in Honduras, write, "People are often joyful and delighted in some of the smallest pleasures of life. Many times the songs the people sing in their daily hardships are songs of hope leading to a better life." The church is working to help create little steps of improvement in the lives of Hondurans and in this way is an agent of Christ's love and mercy. Find Honduras on the map on page 110.

Did You Know?

Mayan people have lived in what is now western Honduras far back before the birth of Jesus. In the early Mayan tradition the first people were made out of corn, which is still a major food of the people of Central America. The people are nourished and their lives are renewed by the very same material that they were made from—corn. Look in Genesis 2:7 to find the Bible story that tells what the first people were made from.

What You Can Do

Organize a book exchange at your church. Ask members of your Sunday school class or the whole congregation to bring in one to three books that are in good condition. Designate a table or area at the church where people can bring their books and browse through other people's offerings. Each book a person brings in may be exchanged for another one on the table. If after a month or so people are finished exchanging books, you can donate the books to a local women's shelter or community center.

Giving What You Have

Is there a preschool or community center in your town that serves children in need? If so, look through your books, coloring supplies, and art supplies for items in almost new condition. Donate these to the center. Don't forget to put something in your Pentecost Offering coin box.

Word of the Week — Endurance

Endurance is having the ability to stick with things or stay committed to something, especially in the face of difficulty.

Prayer

God, you teach us so much and want us to learn. Thank you for the blessings of my school. Be with children who have no schools. Help your church to work in mission to bring schools to children in need. Amen.

MISSION IN THE UNITED STATES

Presbytery of San Juan

Puerto Rico

You probably know that Puerto Rico is not a U.S. state, but did you know it is a commonwealth associated with the United States? That means it has its own government but has decided to be connected with the United States. Puerto Ricans are considered U.S. citizens, but they don't get to vote in the presidential elections and they don't get to pay U.S. income taxes! If you look on the map on page 110, you will find Puerto Rico just to the east of Haiti and the Dominican Republic and north of Venezuela. It's in the Caribbean Sea. On the map on page 112 you'll see a box in the lower right that shows the Synod of Puerto Rico. If you look closely you'll see San Juan Presbytery in the northern part of the island.

Two of the churches in this presbytery are connecting with older adults. Hato Rey Presbyterian Church sponsors a group of women who are 65 years or older and who are volunteers in their church and community. They like to do things for other people, and so they take people without cars to places like the doctor and the grocery store. They work with children, run a recycling program, and do many other things. Another church works with older people who are having a hard time themselves. The church provides breakfast and lunch to these older adults who are homeless or poor. These two churches and other Puerto Rican churches welcome people of all ages and of all abilities to give and to receive.

Did You Know?

Besides Puerto Rico, the Northern Mariana Islands are an official U.S. commonwealth. These two commonwealths are not to be confused with four U.S. states that call themselves commonwealths: Kentucky, Massachusetts, Pennsylvania, and Virginia.

Scripture

As they were going along the road, someone said to him, "I will follow you wherever you go." And Jesus said to him, "Foxes have holes, and birds of the air have nests; but the Son of Man has nowhere to lay his head" (Luke 9:57–58).

Recipe

Picana de Pollo (Chicken Stew)

This is a festive holiday meal in Bolivia.

Ingredients

6–8 chicken breasts, boneless
1/2 cup frozen green peas
1 bay leaf
1 small onion, chopped small
1 8-oz. can tomato paste
3 carrots cut in slices
1 tsp. chili pepper powder
1/8 tsp. dried thyme
1 stalk of celery, chopped
1/4 cup finely chopped parsley
1 tsp. black pepper
1 1/2 tsp. salt
2 cups water
2 chicken bouillon cubes
8 white potatoes, peeled
2 cups frozen corn

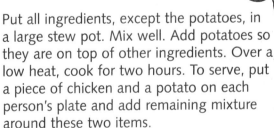

Put all ingredients, except the potatoes, in a large stew pot. Mix well. Add potatoes so they are on top of other ingredients. Over a low heat, cook for two hours. To serve, put a piece of chicken and a potato on each person's plate and add remaining mixture around these two items.

MISSION AROUND THE WORLD

Bolivia

Many children and young adults of Cochambamba, Bolivia, have no home to go to and instead live on the streets. They are struggling each day, facing life with few opportunities and little comfort. Amid their challenging situation sits Madre de Dios, a safe, welcoming home for many of the homeless children, youth, and women of Cochambamba. It is supported by a grant from the PC(USA)'s Hunger Program and run by the Amanecer Foundation, a partner organization of the PC(USA). Half of those served by Madre de Dios ("Mother of God" in Spanish) are under twelve years of age. Here the children have a place to live and attend school. Mothers have the opportunity to be trained for jobs and have time to look for jobs while their children are cared for.

Each person who enters Madre de Dios is treated with respect and kindness by a staff who helps them do what they need to do—get training, see a doctor or dentist, find a permanent home, or get help for drug problems. Many in the city do not realize the number of children who are living on the streets. But Madre de Dios is creating a haven. While many people might turn away from a young child asking for coins on the corner, Madre de Dios

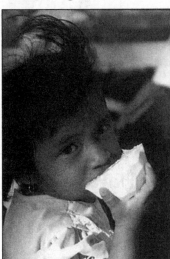

is offering such children warm food to eat, clean water to drink, and beds to sleep in. The people who work at this safe place see the children of Bolivia who seem invisible to many and with compassion and Christ's love make them visible once again.

Children are cared for while mothers have the opportunity to be trained for jobs.

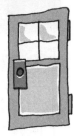

Word of the Week — Home

H – *hearth and heart*
O – *open arms to hug*
M – *memories and traditions*
E – *easy place to be yourself*

Prayer

O God, I thank you for my home and its comforts. Today, be with those who have no home. By your Spirit help us to care and work for those without homes so that all your children know the comforts of home. Amen.

Next Sunday is Pentecost Sunday. Find out more about the first Pentecost by reading the minute for mission in the Mission Yearbook for Prayer & Study. *Look on the page for May 15.*

What You Can Do

On a piece of paper draw an outline of your room. Now draw in your bed, dresser, and other items in your room. Also put in special things that stay in your room: pictures, stuffed animals, and other items that mean a lot to you. Now imagine you are having to leave your home. You have a regular-sized backpack and you can only take the five or six things from your room that will fit in your backpack. Everything else will have to be left behind, and you will have to carry your backpack full of these items with you everywhere you go. What will you take and why do you choose these items?

Giving What You Have

Next Sunday is Pentecost, the day many churches receive the Pentecost Offering. Part of the money from that offering will go to children at risk of, among other things, being homeless. For every room in your home, put 25 cents in your coin box.

Pentecost Offering

MISSION IN THE UNITED STATES

Presbytery of the James

Virginia

Rockfish Presbyterian Church in Nellysford, Virginia, uses its share of the Pentecost Offering to send young people in the community to summer camps. Nellysford is a rural area where many young people have not traveled too far from home. Often they live in houses needing repair. Some come from homes that still do not have indoor plumbing. Rockfish Presbyterian sends younger children to county recreational summer day programs and older elementary children and adolescents to overnight and adventure camp at Hanover Presbytery Camp and Brown's Summit Youth Camp. As one young man said when he learned he was going to camp this year in a neighboring state, "I've never been out of state in my whole life!" For him and for many others, the spirit of Pentecost is felt in the offering of new breath and new life through summer camp.

Rockfish Presbyterian Church is in the Presbytery of the James. Find the presbytery on the map on page 112.

With help from the Pentecost Offering, Rockfish Presbyterian Church helps children get a breath of fresh air.

Scripture

"As the Father has sent me, so I send you" (John 20:21b).

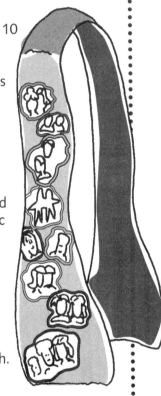

Craft

Pentecost Stole

Create a "Pentecost stole" for your pastor. You can do this by yourself, with other family members, with a church school class, or with friends.

☀ Get a strip of fabric about 10 feet long and somewhere between 4 and 6 inches wide. You can sew sections of cloth together if you need to.
☀ Ask an adult in your family for help in copying a current photo directory of your church.
☀ Cut out several photos and arrange them on the fabric strip, leaving a foot-long section in the middle empty.
☀ Paste the photos on the fabric strip and let dry.
☀ Decorate the edges of the photos with puffy paint to help bond them to the cloth.
☀ Fold it up carefully and wrap it as a gift to your pastor.

Giving What You Have

Create a nature card for someone who would enjoy a breath of "new life." Look outdoors for things that catch your eye: a pretty leaf, a piece of bark, a nice stone, or whatever you find. Glue them onto a piece of paper and write a note of encouragement or thanks to that person.

Did You Know?

On the first Day of Pentecost the Spirit came and helped the disciples find courage and hope. The Spirit gave the disciples the ability to share the story of God's love in languages they had never learned. Because of this amazing action everyone who was gathered in Jerusalem could understand and respond to what the disciples were saying. Today, almost 2,000 years since the first Pentecost, the Holy Spirit is still working to support us in our hope and to make amazing things happen. Through the Pentecost Offering we are part of the Spirit's work as we bring and restore hope to children at risk, youth, and young adults. Forty percent of the Pentecost Offering is kept by local congregations to help children in their community. The remaining 60 percent is used by the General Assembly to help children and give young people opportunities to learn about church leadership.

Prayer

Dear God, thank you for sending the Holy Spirit to bring new life to us. Thank you for the Spirit that brings and holds us together as God's people. When things get difficult sometimes, remind us that you are with us and will never leave us. In Jesus' name. Amen.

MISSION AROUND THE WORLD
Philippines

Is Tagalog a subject in school in the United States?" asked a young Filipino boy. Young Adult Volunteer Sarah Tuttle replied, "No." The boy then asked, "Why not? In our school we have to learn both Tagalog and English." Sarah had a hard time explaining to him why he had to learn her language in school but she didn't have to learn his!

Obet is 14. He has a wide grin that attracts many new friends. He lives with his family across from the church. When Sarah walks out of the church doors each evening to go home, he often will stop her to chat—he in his broken English, Sarah in her broken Tagalog. Sarah thinks about the day when he will ask, "After you go back to the United States in August, when will you return here? Will you miss us?"

"Conversations like these are one of the many reasons I believe God has called me here: to learn the stories of the people God has created so lovingly," writes Sarah. She appreciates the opportunity to learn about the Philippines and is glad to have the chance to see her own world and God's world from a new point of view. Money from the Pentecost Offering gives young adults like Sarah the chance to learn about how God's people all around the world are part of our family.

PENTECOST OFFERING

What You Can Do

☀ The Day of Pentecost is also called the birthday of the church. Ask your teacher if you can have a birthday party for the church in your church school class. Form a circle and hold hands as a reminder that together we are all part of God's family.

☀ The Republic of the Philippines is composed of over 7,000 tropical islands. Find them on the map on page 111.

☀ Read letters from Young Adult Volunteers like Sarah that are posted on the Web site www.pcusa.org/missionconnections/yav.htm to learn more about short-term mission service.

Word of the Week Special Offering

The special offerings—One Great Hour of Sharing, Pentecost, Peacemaking, and Christmas Joy—are four opportunities during the church year for Presbyterians to help God's people. The offerings were created by the General Assembly of the Presbyterian Church (U.S.A.) so that Presbyterians can have the chance to give to specific missions of the church in addition to their regular giving.

MISSION IN THE UNITED STATES

Southwest Presbytery

Puerto Rico

What happens if your church doesn't have a pastor? Who preaches? Who leads the church? Many Presbyterian churches have a good solution: train church members who aren't pastors and let them preach and lead the church. In Puerto Rico, Southwest Presbytery is doing just that. It started a lay school, which trains people who are not pastors. The lay school helps people who attend learn to be better leaders and teachers in the church. The school in Southwest Presbytery takes two years. Some of the people who attended the lay school are thinking about becoming pastors. They are called *inquirers,* and they spend time studying, praying, and talking with people who help them understand if God wants them to be pastors. Those who have decided to become pastors must go to even more school! Sister Idalmy Matos-Rodríguez is one of the students in the lay school who is going to become a pastor. She is now attending the Evangelical Seminary of Puerto Rico, where she will learn to be a pastor. Southwest Presbytery is proud of these students and the churches are happy to have them be their leaders. Find Southwest Presbytery on the map on page 112.

Did You Know?

A layperson is someone who has not been ordained as a minister. A lay pastor is a pastor who hasn't been ordained. So lay schools are for people who want to serve God but don't necessarily want to be ordained. Layperson comes from a Greek word that means "people."

Scripture

The gifts Christ gave were that some would be apostles, some prophets, some evangelists, some pastors and teachers, to equip the saints for the work of ministry, for building up the body of Christ (Ephesians 4:11–12).

Craft

Caretas (Papier-mâché Masks)

One of the most popular craft items in Puerto Rico are the *caretas,* or papier-mâché masks worn during parades and carnivals. These masks can be made of any color but always include many horns, fang teeth, and half-animal, half-human characteristics. Make your own mask by following one of these sets of directions:

☀ You can make a mask by purchasing a mask form at a local craft center and decorating it with paint, feathers, and other items. Just be sure to get craft glue that will stick to the surface of the mask.

☀ Or you can use a balloon, papier-mâché materials purchased at a craft center, and newspaper. Blow the balloon up and tie it. Cut the newspaper into long, thin strips. Follow the directions on the papier-mâché package for mixing the materials. Then dip the newspaper strips one at a time into the mixture, coating them well, and gently wrap the coated newspaper strips around the balloon. Once the balloon is coated, you can add papier-mâché horns, noses, and other desired features. Let dry completely. When the strips are dry, pop the balloon inside and cut the remaining shape in half, so you can use one half as a mask. Paint the mask and add feathers or other decorations.

MISSION AROUND THE WORLD

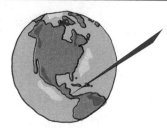

Costa Rica

Sara and Guido Mahecha have been partners in mission with Presbyterian churches in Latin America for over 30 years. Currently they are serving in Costa Rica. Can you find Costa Rica on the map on page 110? Sara and Guido work at the Latin American Biblical University in San José. This university has other centers in places like Guatemala and Bolivia. These centers offer programs that allow students to study while keeping their jobs, living with their families, and working with their own churches. The program encourages students to try out what they are learning by bringing new ideas and activities to their churches. Before they went to the Latin American Biblical University, Sara and Guido served in Colombia, Bolivia, and Brazil. They are pleased with the wide variety of mission work the PC(USA) does in Latin America and the support that the church gives to mission overseas.

Sara Mahecha leads a workshop in Dallas, Texas.

Word of the Week

Ministry

Ministry is our service to God. All of us do ministry when we do things for God.

Prayer

God, you want everyone to know you and to belong to a loving community. Help those who are building new churches to make places that welcome everyone, allow children to have fun, and teach the story of Jesus to people of all ages. Show me how I can do ministry for you. In Jesus' name. Amen.

Giving What You Have

Think about the best church school teacher you have had. Why was that person the best? What did he or she teach you? Ask your parents or siblings who they consider their best church school teacher and what that person taught them about faith, the Bible, or God. Write a thank-you note to your current church school teacher.

What You Can Do

Find out how good you are at teaching yourself or someone else to do something. Read the Scripture verse for this week. See if you can memorize it. You may want to write it out several times or read one phrase at a time, then cover it and recite it aloud. See how long it takes you to memorize the verse. Now help someone else. Is it easier to teach yourself or someone else? Did you enjoy teaching?

MISSION IN THE UNITED STATES

Northwest Presbytery

Puerto Rico

If you could create your very own city, what would you include? Would you have candy stores and skate parks? Would you take care of the medical needs of your citizens? Think about it for a moment. What would be important to include? The churches who are members of Northwest Presbytery in Puerto Rico now have the opportunity both to imagine what they would include in a city and to start building this city! Through an organization called the Presbiterianos en Servicio a la Comunidad, or PESAC (Presbyterians in Community Services), the presbytery is helping to develop a "city" on 14 acres of land. The plan includes five projects: 50 places for older adults to live, including older adults who are now homeless; a home for abused children; a center that helps people with HIV/AIDS; 22 apartments for persons with disabilities; and a community program with a day-care center for older adults.

PESAC and the presbytery are working together to find funding from the government, private agencies, and the church. The vision for a caring community that reaches those who often get overlooked is being made real through their partnership and the support from the surrounding community. Find Northwest Presbytery in Puerto Rico on the map on page 112.

Word of the Week Respect

When you respect someone, you see him or her as a person of worth, and that person's opinions and choices are as important as yours. You can respect someone without agreeing with him or her.

Scripture

"Let the little children come to me, and do not stop them; for it is to such as these that the kingdom of God belongs" (Luke 18:16).

Recipe

Venezuelan Cachapas (Corn Cakes)

You'll need a blender and a griddle; or you can use a mixer and a large frying pan. When you are using any of these, please make sure you ask for help before you begin.

Ingredients

Cooking spray or shortening
2 16-oz. cans of corn
1/2 tsp. salt
1 egg
1/2 cup sugar
3/4 cup whole milk

Put all ingredients in the blender and blend on high for 2 minutes. Check the mixture. It should be thick but not too lumpy. If you find your mixture is too thin, add a small amount of flour or more corn. Once the mixture is somewhat thick, drop a big spoonful of it onto a preheated griddle or frying pan that has been lightly coated with cooking spray or shortening. Cook pancakes approximately 1 1/2 minutes each side or until the side is bubbling. Serve these corn cakes hot and with shredded or crumbled cheese on top.

What You Can Do

Talk with your family about ways you show respect for one another. Are there ways in which anyone thinks he or she is not respected? How does that feel? What are ways you show respect for friends? This week be conscious of the ways you show respect to people at school, church, and home.

People in Venezuela are making changes so that their children's future may be bright.

Giving What You Have

How many weeks will you have of summer vacation? For each week, put 10 cents in the offering plate on Sunday. Remember that your regular offering helps your church continue to do important ministry.

MISSION AROUND THE WORLD

Venezuela

Does everyone in your Sunday school agree on everything? Do you all like the same songs? Does everyone like to do the special projects? Does everyone like to read out loud? People who study together and worship together don't have to agree on everything. Politics is something that people have very different thoughts and feelings about. In some churches you don't talk about politics because you don't want people to get angry and upset. In Venezuela, however, the churches do talk about politics because it is so important to the well-being of the country.

Venezuela is one of the oldest and strongest democratic countries in its region. Find this country on the map on page 110. The discovery of oil gave it a strong economy. But it also opened the gates for greed and corruption in the government. Some people are unhappy with the government and hold protests and strikes. The Presbyterian Church of Venezuela works hard to promote respect between members with different political views. While local church pastors work to keep peace within their congregations, their hope for the future is that change for the better can take place in their churches as well as in the country. As members of the churches learn to listen, hear, and respect one another, they can go out into their communities to offer Christ's ministry of justice and love.

Did You Know?

Venezuela has the fastest growing population in South America. Currently half the people living in Venezuela are under the age of 18!

MISSION IN THE UNITED STATES

The Presbytery of San Joaquin

California

You've heard of the 12 Days of Christmas, but you probably haven't heard of the "12 Days of Mission"! First Presbyterian Church in Visalia, California, just finished its second "12 Days of Mission" and is ready to make it an annual event. This mission program gave more than 200 people of all ages and backgrounds the chance to work on mission projects both in their own town and in some places outside the United States. Volunteers were very enthusiastic about the mission work.

There were over 20 ministry projects from which to choose. The volunteers signed up on Sunday and they were busy for the next 12 days. They helped with homework at the Boys & Girls Club,

Scripture

The needy shall not always be forgotten, nor the hope of the poor perish forever (Psalm 9:18).

played games at a school partnership program, worked at a shelter for homeless people, cooked at a soup kitchen, helped in a Rescue Mission thrift store, and prayed with people recovering from addictions. Volunteers who wanted to work in another country were able to get involved with mission workers in Germany, Australia, Mexico, Guatemala, and Paraguay. Many who served during the 12 days have continued to volunteer on a regular basis. As people gathered for worship following the 12 days, they told stories of how their own lives had been enriched by reaching out to help someone else. "The Spirit of God blessed us too," concluded one volunteer.

Game

Help Tom fight the causes of hunger in Peru. Get a family member or a friend to play this game with you. Use two buttons or dimes as your playing pieces. Use a penny as your dice. Toss the penny: heads you move two spaces, tails you move one space.

Did You Know?

The Appalachian Trail was built by volunteers. Today it is still maintained mostly by volunteers. Want to volunteer to help keep this 2,173-mile trail in good order? You don't have to have any experience building trails: you just have to be willing to work hard and get dirty!

MISSION AROUND THE WORLD

Peru

How far would you be willing to walk to fight poverty? One mile? 10 miles? 100 miles? How about 2,173 miles? Tom Geiger has worked most of his life fighting poverty all over the world, including in Peru. When Tom heard about the work Joining Hands Against Poverty Network of Peru was doing, he wanted to help. Joining Hands-Peru is a mission of the Presbyterian Hunger Program. It has been doing many things to make the lives of people in Peru better, like getting the works of artists in Peru to places where they can sell for enough money that the artists can support themselves. It's also been helping the people in the village of La Oroya to fight a U.S. factory located there whose pollution has caused the people to become ill. And it works for human rights in Peru.

Tom volunteered to have his own one-man walkathon to raise money for and awareness about Joining Hands-Peru. His idea was to hike the Appalachian Trail, which is 2,173 miles long from northeast Georgia to Mount Katahdin, Maine, most of it in mountains. Tom asked people to pledge money for each mile he walked. They did, and he started walking in April 2004. He made it to the end of the trail in September, tired but happy that he could help Joining Hands-Peru. Find Peru on the map on page 110.

Prayer

God, I don't really know what it's like to not have enough food. Help me to be aware of people who go hungry. Help me to do whatever I can to keep people from being hungry. Give strength to those who are hungry. In Jesus' name. Amen.

Tom Geiger (left) walked more than 2,000 miles to raise funds for Joining Hands-Peru.

What You Can Do

Volunteer to do something for someone this week. Does someone in your family need help doing something you can do? Do it because you choose to. (It doesn't count if a parent asks you!) After you have volunteered, think about how it feels to volunteer to do something.

Word of the Week   Volunteer

Volunteers are people who do things to help others just because they want to help and they enjoy helping others. Volunteers are never paid for giving their time and help.

Giving What You Have

Remember the suggested New Year's resolution about writing someone like a mission co-worker (see page 4)? Bring happiness to that person by writing him or her.

MISSION IN THE UNITED STATES

Presbytery of San José

California

Do you speak Spanish? Let's say you know some Spanish, and you have a friend who speaks Spanish and only a little English. So you are going to teach your friend some English. On the day you have decided to meet for the lesson, your friend shows up with some of his or her friends who also want to learn to speak more English. But they don't speak Spanish: they speak German, Japanese, and Korean!

Something like that happened to the Westminster Presbyterian Church in San José. For a few years, a group of people who spoke Spanish had met as the Latin American Fellowship in the chapel of Westminster Church. But they had few members, so together with the Westminster Church they decided to be one church with two languages. They hired a new minister to be director of Hispanic Ministries, and she and her husband started teaching English as a second language as a service to the church and community. They were expecting people who spoke Spanish and who lived in the neighborhood to come to the classes. And Spanish-speaking people did come. What the teachers didn't expect were the people from Germany, Japan, Korea, and Vietnam who also came! Instead of two languages, several languages could be heard in the class. The church was glad to have everyone come and didn't mind the surprise at all. Westminster Presbyterian Church is in the Presbytery of San José. Find this presbytery on the map on page 112.

What You Can Do

Is there someone in your school, neighborhood, or church who speaks a language other than English? If so, find out how to say "hello" in that language and then greet that person. Ask him or her to teach you some other words or phrases.

HOLA!

Scripture

"Whoever welcomes one such child in my name welcomes me" (Matthew 18:5).

Craft

Mayan Pendant

Native people of Colombia make pendants out of coal using Mayan designs. Make one for yourself.

Materials

2-inch square cut from poster board
black crayon
nail
scissors
18-inch piece of black yarn or cord
hole punch

Color the whole square of poster board with the black crayon, bearing down hard so the color is dark. Cut a circle from the square by rounding off the corners. Make a hole in the middle of the circle with the hole punch. Using the nail as a pencil, draw one of the patterns shown on the circle, bearing down hard enough so you can see the lines your nail makes. When you are through, fold the yarn or string in half, thread the midpoint of the yarn—where the fold is—through the hole in the black circle. Then place the two ends of yarn through the loop you've just made and pull them all the way through. Tie the two ends of yarn together so you can put the pendant around your neck.

MISSION AROUND THE WORLD

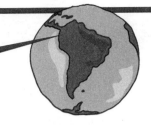

Colombia

The PC(USA) is very concerned about all the killing and violence in Colombia and about the millions of people who have fled their homes and now live in camps. And because anyone who works with these people, called displaced persons, can also be in danger, the PC(USA) is very concerned about the pastors and other workers trying to help them. Many pastors and workers have been put in jail, kidnapped, and even killed. Rick Ufford-Chase, moderator of the 216th General Assembly (2004), went to Colombia in September 2004 to accompany the Rev. Milton Mejia, the executive secretary of the Presbyterian Church of Colombia. The two visited several government leaders to tell them of the PC(USA)'s concern. While sitting in the office of a government official, Milton got a call on his cell phone and learned of the killing of a friend who had been working with the displaced persons and had been jailed because of his work. He had just gotten out of jail a few days earlier. Now he had been killed.

Milton has asked the PC(USA) to send some people from the United States to be accompaniers—to go with the church people wherever they go and to watch what the government, the army, and other fighting groups are doing. They can bring a little more safety to the church people just by being there and bringing to the attention of people around the world the things that are happening in Colombia. For the short time Rick was there, he was an accompanier. Now the PC(USA) is bringing other people to Colombia to be accompaniers. Find Colombia on the map on page 110.

Alexa Smith

Church people in Colombia are working with people like this boy who lives in a displaced persons' camp.

Did You Know?

Milton Mejia grew up in a poor neighborhood. His parents did not go to church, but they sent him to a church school. There he learned about Jesus Christ. Soon he was attending church and loving it. He became active in the youth group as soon as he was old enough to join. His gift of leadership did not go unnoticed. He preached his first sermon in a Sunday morning worship service when he was 13. That was over 20 years ago. Now he is the executive secretary of the Presbyterian Church of Colombia.

Word of the Week **Accompanier**

When you accompany someone, you go along with that person wherever he or she is going. In the special sense used in the story about Colombia, an accompanier goes with someone who is in danger; and just by the accompanier's presence, the person may be in less danger.

Giving What You Have

How many languages can you say "hello" or "good-bye" in? Probably more than you realize. For every language you can say "hello" or "good-bye" in, put 10 cents in the offering plate on Sunday.

ADIOS!

Prayer

People around the world pray to God in their own languages. God understands all languages. Prayer is more about the thoughts of our hearts and minds, not about language. Pray the Lord's Prayer by just humming. Concentrate on the meaning and feelings. Even without words you are praying!

Word of the Week — Literacy

Literacy comes from a Latin word that means "letter." Knowing your letters is the first step in learning how to read. A literacy class teaches people to read.

MISSION IN THE UNITED STATES

Presbytery of Boise

Idaho, Nevada, Oregon

The PC(USA) has two mission areas: Snake River Mission Area and the Sierra Mission Partnership. These mission areas were set up to cover large areas of the western United States that don't have a lot of people. Most of the towns are small, and so are the churches. In the Snake River Mission Area three presbyteries work together. One of the problems they have faced is that the small churches can't afford to have pastors. The three presbyteries of Snake River—the Presbyteries of Boise, Eastern Oregon, and Kendall—came up with a solution: teach lay people how to lead the services (see the Did You Know? on page 46 if you have forgotten what a layperson is). The Presbytery of Boise started the Seminary Without Walls five years ago with two students. So far four lay people have completed the program, and now there's a class of 12 with people from other churches besides Presbyterians. The churches of the Presbytery of Boise and the other presbyteries of Snake River Mission Area will continue to have dedicated leaders to serve them. Find the Presbytery of Boise on the map on page 112.

Scripture

Search me, O God, and know my heart; test me and know my thoughts. See if there is any wicked way in me, and lead me in the way everlasting (Psalm 139:23–24).

Recipe

Brazilian Feyoada Rice

Ask an adult to help you make this recipe.

Ingredients
3 tbs. oil
1 1/2 cups rice
1 onion, peeled and sliced
1 14.5-oz. can tomatoes
1 4.5-oz. can green chilies
1 1/2 cups canned beef broth
1/2 cups golden raisins
1 1/2 tsp. salt

Heat the oil in a skillet. Add rice and onion and cook for 10 minutes over a very low heat. Add the tomatoes and chilies. Slowly pour the beef broth in. Add the raisins and salt. Bring the rice to a boil, then cook on low heat for 20 to 25 minutes.

MISSION AROUND THE WORLD

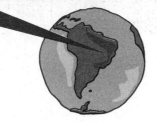

Brazil

Some congregations project the words to hymns or prayers in the front of the sanctuary so everyone can see. What a great idea! It saves paper because nothing has to be printed and it keeps people looking up instead of down at their bulletins. They do this in the congregation where Farris and Thelma Goodrum worship—the Independent Presbyterian Church in Londrina, Brazil. But one day Thelma noticed that some of the adults in the congregation were standing quietly, embarrassed because they could not read. She helped the church organize an adult literacy class. The students were excited. "Oh, it is so good to finally be able to read and write!" one of them shouted after attending classes. What made Thelma the happiest was watching the students in church after they had finished the class. They were able to participate just like everyone else—reading the words and singing the songs with joy.

Young members of a Brazilian congregation in Itabuna raise their voices in song.

Did You Know?

June 19 is Father's Day. The first Father's Day was observed on June 19, 1910, in Spokane, Washington. Mrs. John B. Dodd of Washington wanted to honor her father because of the way he had brought up his children after his wife had died. Other people decided they wanted to celebrate a father's day. It wasn't until 1966 that the third Sunday of June became the official Father's Day in the United States.

Prayer

God of love, bless me and my friends when we play. Keep us safe when we play and help us to play fair and enjoy each other. When we laugh and have a good time may we always remember to be thankful to you. Amen.

Did You Know?

More than 20 percent of adults in the United States read at or below a fifth-grade level. Because they can't read well, these adults have a hard time finding jobs that pay well.

Giving What You Have

For every special class you have taken or program you have attended at your church this year, put 25 cents in your church's offering plate this week.

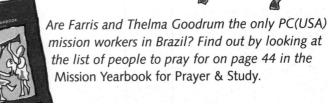

Are Farris and Thelma Goodrum the only PC(USA) mission workers in Brazil? Find out by looking at the list of people to pray for on page 44 in the Mission Yearbook for Prayer & Study.

What You Can Do

Think about all the things you can do because you can read. What a great tool reading is! Spend some time reading with a younger brother, sister, or friend who hasn't learned to read.

Word of the Week

June 26–July 2

Scripture

Hymn

A hymn is a song of praise to God.

Praise the LORD! Sing to the LORD a new song, his praise in the assembly of the faithful (Psalm 149:1).

MISSION IN THE UNITED STATES

Presbytery of New Brunswick

New Jersey

Life is a lot more fun when you find a friend who enjoys the same things you do! Two boys in New Jersey have become great friends while singing God's praises in the Trenton Children's Chorus. One of the first things the two boys do in choir practice is warm up their voices. See if you can warm up your voice with Kurt and Nathaniel. Put your arms up and place your hands behind your head. Use your stomach muscles to push the air out of your mouth as you make a "choo" sound like a train. Say "choo" eight times and then end with a long "choo-o-o," sending all the air out. Now sigh, shrugging your shoulders and arms down to your sides. Sigh again, this time starting on a very high note and sliding down as low as you can go.

The Trenton Children's Chorus, which is supported by the Presbytery of New Brunswick, brings young people from different backgrounds together not only to make music but also to learn about each other. Nathaniel lives in Trenton, New Jersey, and Kurt lives in Princeton, which is not far away. Nathaniel and Kurt first got to know each other through singing in the choir. They became friends and have done other things together. Nathaniel stayed with Kurt when Kurt's church had a day camp in the summer. Then the two roomed together on a choir trip to Boston. They enjoy seeing each other when they can. And they enjoy what brought them together in the first place—singing! Find the Presbytery of New Brunswick on the map on page 112.

Puzzle
Hymn Writing

Fill in a word or words that will complete this message as a hymn, poem, or prayer. You don't have to make words rhyme. When you are finished filling in the blanks, use a familiar tune and try to put the phrases to music.

O God, you are the maker
of _____ and
_____ .
Your hands have placed the
_____ in the
_____ .
At your word the
_____ were made
And your fingers stretched the
_____ .
Even the _____
obeys your voice.
Lord, you fill me with
_____ .
I am _____
with you.

Nathaniel and Kurt enjoy singing in the Trenton Children's Chorus.

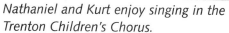

Prayer

If you have a hymnbook at home, look in it for a favorite hymn. If you don't have one, think of a hymn you know. Read or recite the words of the hymn slowly as a prayer. Think about the words you are saying. Read or recite the verse twice.

Giving What You Have

Do you have *The Presbyterian Hymnal* at your home? If not, ask your family if you can pool some of your money and purchase one (they are about $12). If your home already has a hymnal, consider purchasing one for your church to give to a person who joins the church and is a new Presbyterian. At home you can use a hymnal to pray the hymns, learn about the church, and better understand our faith.

MISSION AROUND THE WORLD

Ethiopia

The Anuak people of western Ethiopia live in villages beside rivers and raise sheep and goats. They also farm and fish. When their land can no longer grow crops, they move to nearby places with fertile soil. The church is strong among the Anuak people. One reason for its strength is that when missionaries first came to this part of Africa, they translated the New Testament into the Anuak language. Soon the Anuak people will have the complete Bible in their language. Marie Lusted, a mission worker in Gambella, Ethiopia, has lived with the Anuak since 1955. She has been translating parts of the Old Testament for the past twenty years. Whenever a new book of the Bible is completed in the Anuak language, she is very excited. "The Word of God is alive and powerful," she writes. "It has guided the church in Ethiopia and provided instruction and comfort." And, she adds, it inspires people to write new hymns.

Find Ethiopia on the map on page 111.

What You Can Do

Look through *The Presbyterian Hymnal* and find the section about Church. You'll find the section names at the top left and right on all the pages. You'll find three subsections under Church: Mission, Universal, and Triumphant. If you have trouble finding the sections on Church, go to the back of the hymnal to the Topical Index that starts on page 691 and look under "Church." Choose a hymn title that sounds interesting and read the words of the hymn. What do the words of this hymn tell you about the church? Why might the hymn writer have thought these words were important for people to sing? Does singing help you remember the words better? How do hymns help us remember how to be God's people?

General Assembly

Understanding the General Assembly

Scripture

"Come to me, all you that are weary and are carrying heavy burdens, and I will give you rest" (Matthew 11:28).

Have you ever thought about how the PC(USA) works? You can see how things work in your own congregation: the session meets and makes a decision, a committee or work group is formed, and then people get to work to make things happen!

In fact, the way we work is so important that our name comes from a very old Greek word for elder: *presbyter*. When your congregation needs to choose leaders, it elects members to the session. Everyone on the session is an elder—a *presbyter*—and all of them are specially called by God to be leaders in the church. The session takes care of the church—looking after the staff, the programs, and the building. Most sessions meet once a month.

It isn't so much different at the presbytery and synod. Take a look at the map on page 112 and see the boundaries for presbyteries and synods. Presbyteries are made up of lots of churches; synods are made up of several presbyteries; and the General Assembly, when it meets, includes people from all of them.

When a presbytery, a geographical group of many congregations, needs to make decisions, the congregations send commissioners to a presbytery meeting. Commissioners are elders who are representatives from their congregations. A representative is someone who speaks and acts for a larger group of people. The people who can vote at a meeting of the presbytery are elder-commissioners and all of the ministers in the presbytery. The elder-commissioners and ministers meet, discuss important plans, and vote how they sense the Holy Spirit is leading them. Most presbyteries meet several times a year.

When the whole PC(USA) denomination meets, the meeting is called a General Assembly. Commissioners to a General Assembly are representatives from their presbyteries: ministers and elders. Presbyteries choose and send commissioners to the General Assembly every other year to make decisions about how the PC(USA) is going to work.

At the General Assembly, people meet in small groups to study, pray, and talk about the decisions that need to be made. Then they meet in one very large group and vote on the decisions. But that isn't the end of it! Some of the decisions are so important that the people at the General Assembly aren't the only ones who decide. That's when they tell the presbyteries that they need to vote. So the overtures (that just means ideas to vote on) are sent to the presbyteries from the General Assembly, and the commissioners at the presbytery meeting vote. Then the votes of all the presbyteries are added up and the decision is made!

This is a lot like how the U.S. government works. There are town councils and city and county governments, then state legislatures, and then the federal government. Each one has its own special work to do. Different areas of a state send their representatives to the state capital, and each state sends representatives to the national capital.

It is easy to see why it is important to pray for the people and the work of the General Assembly when they meet. Ask God to give them wisdom, courage, and strength as they do the hard work of leading our denomination.

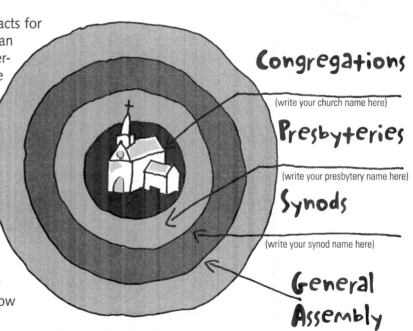

Congregations
(write your church name here)

Presbyteries
(write your presbytery name here)

Synods
(write your synod name here)

General Assembly

Words of the Week

Presbyter, Congregation, Presbytery, Synod, General Assembly

Did You Know?

The 215th General Assembly (2003) made a decision that future General Assembly meetings would take place every other year, with 2005 being the first year without an assembly meeting. The 216th General Assembly took place in 2004 in Richmond, Virginia, and the 217th Assembly will take place in June 2006 in Birmingham, Alabama.

What You Can Do

⊚ Find your presbytery and synod on the map on page 112.

⊚ In the days, weeks, and months between General Assembly meetings, the General

Assembly Council (GAC) meets to follow up on actions and decisions made by the General Assembly. You can read about the GAC on page 261 of the *2005 Mission Yearbook for Prayer & Study*.

⊚ Most synods and presbyteries have a Web site. You can look up your synod and presbytery's Web site by visiting www.pcusa.org/links/pressynod.htm. Find out what ways your presbytery and synod are involved in mission.

⊚ Your own church is represented at the meetings of your presbytery through one or more elders chosen by your session as well as any ministers serving your church. Some presbyteries also recognize church educators. You can find out who will be your church's commissioners to the next meeting of the presbytery by asking your pastor or clerk of session. Pray for these persons and the next meeting of your presbytery.

Prayer

Look again at the map of the Presbyterian Church (U.S.A.) presbyteries and synods on page 112. Put your fingers where your presbytery and synod are located, and pray for them. You can use this prayer or something similar to it: *God of history and God of love, work your love and your history through the mission of your church. Guide me and all your people as we serve one another in Jesus' name. Amen.*

Giving What You Have

Our Presbyterian Church (U.S.A.) continues to work according to the decisions made by the 216th General Assembly (2004). Save one cent for each of our church's General Assemblies, and contribute that in your church's offering to support the mission of the whole church.

David Young

The 216th General Assembly (2004) listens to the first two-term moderator, Elder Rick Ufford-Chase, a 40-year-old mission worker from the Southside Presbyterian Church in Tucson, Arizona.

Eastern Korean Presbytery sponsored an "All Good People Praise Festival" in celebration of the 100th anniversary of Korean immigration to the United States in 1903.

MISSION IN THE UNITED STATES

Eastern Korean Presbytery

Nongeographic

Over 120 years ago, American missionaries went to Korea to teach Korean people about Jesus. Today there are more than 12 million Korean Christians! The Korean church continues to grow. Because missionaries nurtured Korean Christians in their faith, Koreans feel that being good stewards of God's love means showing that love to other people in the world. In 2003 the Korean National Council of Churches reported that more than 3,000 mission workers had been sent from Korea to 68 countries in the world.

The Korean American churches in Eastern Korean Presbytery have also been busy sharing the gospel in the world. Recently 14 churches in the region sent mission workers to South America and China. The presbytery plans to send more in the future. The churches in this presbytery are also interested in serving neighbors in their own communities. The "All Good People Praise Festival" was a celebration of the 100th anniversary of Koreans moving to the United States. At the festival Korean Americans praised God for bringing people of different races and cultures together into one church in Christ. The presbytery invited several church choirs to participate in a special concert and welcomed people from neighboring communities to join the festivities.

Scripture

"Whoever does the will of God is my brother and sister and mother" (Mark 3:35).

Craft
Leaf Rubbings

Save the leaves you collected from your walk around your neighborhood or a park (see Giving What You Have). Pay attention to the trees. Notice the different types of bark the trees have as well as the different shapes of their leaves. Bring your leaves home and get out some sheets of plain white paper, old newspaper, and crayons or colored pencils. Cover the area you will be working on with the newspaper. Lay the leaves on the newspaper in a design. The leaves can overlap. Now put the white paper on top of the leaves and lightly rub over the leaves with the side of a crayon or colored pencil. See what happens when you rub hard and what happens when you rub softly. You can lift the paper at any time and rearrange the leaves underneath to add to the design. Use different colored crayons or pencils to add to your designs.

What You Can Do

There are about 400 Korean-speaking Presbyterian churches in the PC(USA). The language is different, but the church service is probably a lot like the one in your home church. Check the yellow pages of the phone book to see if there is a Korean Presbyterian church in your area. If there is, ask your pastor or an older person in your house to find out whether it would be possible for you to attend a service on Sunday morning.

MISSION AROUND THE WORLD

Madagascar

Picture yourself walking on a path, dripping wet with the dew from what seems like an endless tangle of tree leaves, stems, and flowers. You are in one of the richest places in nature on the planet. The baobab and octopus trees aren't like the trees you know; the many different lemurs, lizards, and flowers take your breath away. This is Madagascar. Find it on the map on page 111. Madagascar has been able to keep much of its natural beauty until recently. In the last few years all but 25 percent of the forests on the island have been cut down, killing many plants only found on Madagascar and leaving animals without homes.

Mission co-workers Dan and Elizabeth Turk work to make the lives of people better without hurting the environment. "We are excited about working with the Church of Jesus Christ in Madagascar [FJKM]," they write. The FJKM believes that being Christian stewards includes caring for both the physical and the spiritual needs of God's people and caring for all of God's creation. Recently Dan went with a team of others to 30 schools where over 9,000 students were growing trees and learning to take care of the earth. "In the two years of the project," writes Dan, "the greatest successes have been planting trees on the school grounds and helping the parents work better together for common goals." They are learning to be good stewards of the earth.

Prayer

Dear God, there are so many leaves in the world, each one unique and individual. You made and love them all. There are so many people in the world, each one unique and individual. Remind me always of your love for leaves and people and everything you created. Amen.

Word of the Week — Steward

A steward is a person responsible for taking care of the things God has given us. To be good stewards in the church, we care for the earth, nurture one another, support the church, and share God's word with those we meet.

Did You Know?

Madagascar is the fourth largest island in the world (Greenland is the largest). Ninety percent of all known species of lemurs live on the island of Madagascar. A lemur is a monkey-like animal with a long, bushy tail.

Dan Turk works with parents and teachers on an environmental education project.

Giving What You Have

Go on a leaf walk. Walk around your neighborhood or in a park and collect as many different types of leaves as you can find. Put 5 cents in the offering plate on Sunday for each type of leaf you collect.

MISSION IN THE UNITED STATES

Presbytery of Newark

New Jersey

Scripture

Teach me your way, O Lᴏʀᴅ, that I may walk in your truth (Psalm 86:11).

If you enjoy a parade, you might like biking the two blocks from Trinity Presbyterian Church in Montclair, New Jersey, to Nishuane Elementary School on a Wednesday or Thursday afternoon. (The church is in the Presbytery of Newark, which you can find on the map on page 112.) You would see first graders skipping, marching, and walking to the Trinity Church's STARS program. When the children reach the church, the first graders are welcomed by high school students who are there to tutor them, give them a snack, and shower them with lots of love. STARS is an after-school ministry for students who need extra help in two important areas: math and reading. Besides the tutoring, the STARS students get a new understanding of what it means to be a child of God. "There were two students who had never been inside a church building before," recalls the Rev. Allen Shelton, pastor of the church. "They asked for a tour of the sanctuary, and when we showed it to them, they were in awe. It is our prayer that these students will grow to feel at home here and, as they get older, feel like they can walk into church anytime."

The ministry also enriches the high school students who volunteer their time. "Working with these first-graders has helped me spiritually," says Dacier Randolph, a volunteer. "I know that I'm serving Christ when I see a student finally understand a math problem or discover a love for reading. And when one smiles at me or gives me a hug, I know God is smiling, too."

Puzzle: African Message

Find Africa in your atlas or on your globe, or use the map of Africa on pages 110–111. Find answers to the following questions from the map. Write the answers in the blanks. When you are finished you will see a special message in the gray area.

1. What country borders Zambia on the east?
2. What country is northeast of Swaziland and east of Zimbabwe?
3. What country is completely surrounded by South Africa?
4. What country is northeast of Zambia and north of Mozambique?
5. What country is east of Botswana?
6. What country is south of Zambia and also south of Angola?
7. What is the southernmost country in Africa?
8. What country is southwest of Zimbabwe?
9. South of the Central African Republic is the Democratic Republic of the _____ .
10. What country is north of Namibia?
11. What large island is just east of Mozambique?

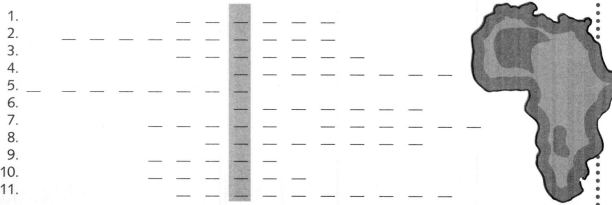

1. ___ ___ ___ ___
2. ___ ___ ___ ___ ___ ___ ___ ___ ___
3. ___ ___ ___ ___ ___ ___ ___ ___
4. ___ ___ ___ ___ ___ ___ ___ ___
5. ___ ___ ___ ___ ___ ___ ___ ___
6. ___ ___ ___ ___ ___ ___ ___
7. ___ ___ ___ ___ ___ ___ ___ ___ ___ ___ ___
8. ___ ___ ___ ___ ___ ___ ___ ___
9. ___ ___ ___ ___ ___
10. ___ ___ ___ ___ ___ ___
11. ___ ___ ___ ___ ___ ___ ___ ___ ___ ___

Answers: 1. Malawi, 2. Mozambique, 3. Lesotho, 4. Tanzania, 5. Zimbabwe, 6. Namibia, 7. South Africa, 8. Botswana, 9. Congo, 10. Angola, 11. Madagascar

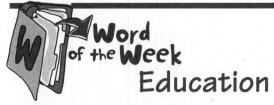

Word of the Week
Education

Education is what you learn in school, in church, and from important people in your life. It is the information and skills you learn to help you live your life well.

Dacier Randolph tutors a young student in the STARS program.

MISSION AROUND THE WORLD
Zambia

Presbyterians have always had a strong interest in education, both in the United States and in other countries. Justo Mwale Theological College is an important part of the educational ministry of the Church of Central Africa Presbyterian, PC(USA)'s partner church in Zambia. Find Zambia on the map on pages 110–111. Chunda Chizason is a student at the college. He is preparing for work as a full-time minister. He has a wife and two young daughters. When he was twenty Chunda attended a revival meeting and decided to become a follower of Christ. He soon became active in the church and started to teach Sunday school. After a year or more he felt God was calling him to be a full-time minister. Though Chunda and his family don't have much money while he is in school, they are grateful to God and to the PC(USA) for the support they receive so that Chunda can stay in school. Soon Chunda will be able to become a pastor in a church.

Find Zambia on the map on pages 110–111.

Prayer

O God, I am a student even though I am on summer vacation now. When I am in school I try my best to learn and study hard. Be with students in schools everywhere. Whether we are in school or on vacation, guide us as we learn so that our minds stay open and alert and so that we may become the people you want us to be. Amen.

What You Can Do

Even if you are not going to school this summer, you are being educated in different ways. Think about something you've learned to do this summer or some information you've learned. Maybe you learned a new way to throw a baseball or a new way to make a friend laugh. Think about ways you have learned something interesting. Tell your parents or an adult friend what you've learned outside of school.

Did You Know?

There are 66 Presbyterian-related colleges in the United States and nine Presbyterian secondary schools.

Giving What You Have

How many days until you go back to school? For each day, put a penny in the offering plate on Sunday.

MISSION IN THE UNITED STATES

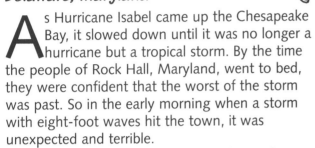

New Castle Presbytery

Delaware, Maryland

As Hurricane Isabel came up the Chesapeake Bay, it slowed down until it was no longer a hurricane but a tropical storm. By the time the people of Rock Hall, Maryland, went to bed, they were confident that the worst of the storm was past. So in the early morning when a storm with eight-foot waves hit the town, it was unexpected and terrible.

Just six weeks earlier, a group from the Presbyterian Church of Chestertown had taken a mission trip to Rocky Mount, North Carolina. The group went to work on homes still in need of repair after Hurricane Floyd had blown through. Chestertown, Maryland, is only 20 miles from Rock Hall. When Hurricane Isabel hit, the mission team wondered if they could provide help to their neighbors in Rock Hall. With money from Presbyterian Disaster Assistance and several thousand dollars from a church member, the mission team reorganized and went to Rock Hall to help rebuild. After attending several town meetings, a project was given to the Chestertown team to work on. This first project opened the door to other projects and more groups coming to help.

Currently the mission team is developing a housing repair ministry in the area around Rock Hall and is working in partnership with the Seventh-Day Adventist Church and the Jewish community.

Word of the Week Connectional

Connectional is how we describe the PC(USA) because of the way everybody and every group connects with each other. Each congregation is connected to the other Presbyterian congregations in the world. Congregations in an area are connected together in presbyteries and then presbyteries are connected into synods. Being connectional makes us more aware of what is happening in other churches and how we can help and support each other.

Scripture

Love one another with mutual affection. . . . If it is possible, so far as it depends on you, live peaceably with all (Romans 12:10, 18).

Craft
Secret Message Decoder
Materials
lemon juice (fresh squeezed works best)
white vinegar
Q-tips
white paper
flashlight or lamp

In some places in the world Christians have to keep their faith a secret or not talk about their church in public. See what it may be like to send a secret message to a church friend. Gather the above supplies and follow these directions:

Put a small amount of lemon juice in one cup and a small amount of vinegar in another cup (about 1 tbs. of each liquid). Think of a message or Scripture verse you want to send your friend. Using the Q-tip like a pen point, dip it in the vinegar and write your message on the white paper. Remember to dip the Q-tip after every letter or every other letter. Now let the paper dry. When the paper is dry you can send your message to a friend. If your friend holds the message up to a lamp or puts a flashlight behind the paper for a while, he or she will be able to read your message. Now take another piece of paper and another Q-tip and use the lemon juice to write with this time!

MISSION AROUND THE WORLD

Angola

Find Angola on the map on pages 110–111. The Presbyterian Church in Angola, like the PC(USA), is a connectional church. This means that one church has ties to the other Presbyterian churches in the country. For Presbyterians both in Angola and in the United States being connected to other churches is very important. So when some churches in Angola lost contact with the rest of the churches, it was difficult for all the churches.

In 1993 a civil war began in Angola. The country became divided into separate areas controlled by different military groups fighting each other. About 20 churches and five presbyteries were cut off from the rest of the churches in Angola. "We felt sad. We had no joy for we could not see our brothers, our colleagues in ministry, the elders, deacons, and those we love," wrote Pastor Antonio Mussaqui. "In some cases we could secretly communicate with a few people in another occupied area. But if the soldiers caught you with a letter from a city outside of their control, a person could be arrested, beaten, and jailed—sometimes even killed." Messages had to be sent secretly. Finally in 2002 the different military groups made peace. People could travel from one city to another. The Presbyterian Church in Angola began contacting one another and reuniting families. At the first big church meeting together they began planning new programs and training workers to go to villages to start new Presbyterian congregations. Angolan Presbyterians were seeing an opportunity to connect their neighbors to the hope of Jesus Christ.

Giving What You Have

Presbyterian Disaster Assistance (PDA) responds to requests by churches and presbyteries for help when hurricanes and other disasters occur. Talk with your church school teacher about having your class collect money and sending it to PDA the next time a disaster destroys homes and businesses. You can go to PDA's Web site at www.pcusa.org/pda to find where and how to send money.

Prayer

Make a list of the people and things you love. Remember to include activities, food, music, friends, and family. Look over your list and think about why you love each person or thing listed. Pray: *God, you are love. Thank you for all the blessings of my life. Thank you especially for . . . (read list). For the joys of my life and life itself, I love and thank you. Amen.*

What You Can Do

Are you prepared for an emergency? Strong storms can leave a home without electricity. Check to see if your home has an emergency kit. The kit should include a working flashlight and extra batteries, candles and matches, one or two gallon jugs of water, some canned goods that don't need to be heated to be eaten, and a working, nonelectric can opener. If your home does have some of these items, you may want to put them together in a plastic box and mark it "Emergency Kit." In case of an emergency, you will know where to find the things you'll need.

Angolans gather at the 5th General Synod meeting of the Presbyterian Church of Angola.

Did You Know

Early Christians were persecuted and needed to hide their faith. They often met in underground cemeteries called catacombs. They drew pictures on the walls of the catacombs that were "secret" messages to other Christians. A peacock meant eternal life; a dove meant peace within your soul; and an anchor meant hope in Jesus.

MISSION IN THE UNITED STATES

Presbytery of Shenandoah

Virginia, West Virginia

"Yo Tango Gozo!"—"I've got the joy down in my heart!" Mission team members from the Presbytery of Shenandoah and the Oaxacan (pronounced wa-HA-kin) people now living in Baja California, Mexico, held hands and sang together in Spanish. And there was joy in the hearts of those singing. Sixty people from 13 churches in the presbytery had come for a week to a town in Mexico where they were helping the Oaxacan native people build houses. People from the Presbytery of Shenandoah had been going there for five years to work on houses and build friendships. (Find this presbytery on the map on page 112.)

The Presbyterians from Shenandoah found out that house building was just one part of the ministry that happened during the week. One of the mission team members, Karen Stevens, said, "What we gave of ourselves during the week in the form of work, fellowship, compassion, and prayers for the families could not compare with what each of us received. We lived, worked, and worshiped with people of faith. We saw the smiles on children's faces when our work van pulled

around a corner. We felt the joy and renewed hope in the adults' handshakes and hospitality." The joy in everyone's heart was great.

Mission trip workers build a house with the Oaxacan community.

Scripture

The LORD is my shepherd, I shall not want. He makes me lie down in green pastures; he leads me beside still waters; he restores my soul (Psalm 23:1–3a).

Recipe

Melkkos (Milk Noodles)

Here's a dish from South Africa that mothers make for their children when they are sick and the mothers want to make sure they will eat something. Ask your mother or another adult to help you make this recipe.

Ingredients

1 8-oz. package of medium egg noodles
6 cups whole milk (2% milk can be substituted)
2 tbs. butter
cinnamon sugar

In a large sauce pan heat milk to a gentle boil. Add egg noodles and butter. Cook on low heat about 20 minutes or until noodles are well cooked. Sprinkle with cinnamon sugar.

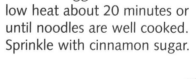

Word of the Week   Heal

To heal is to bring back to health. Sometimes our bodies need healing. Sometimes a friendship needs healing if friends have hurt one another. And sometimes our feelings need healing.

MISSION AROUND THE WORLD

Republic of South Africa

Even when things seem hopeless, God is at work healing, restoring, and bringing a new song to the hearts of those who need it. Cindy Easterday is a PC(USA) mission co-worker in South Africa who works with HIV/AIDS patients and the people who give care to those with HIV/AIDS. Most of the caregivers Cindy trains are volunteers. Sometimes a doctor or nurse will go with the volunteers to see those who are sick, but usually the volunteers go alone. Cindy must prepare the volunteers for what they might see and have to do on the home visits.

In one area volunteers travel over hills to rural towns to deliver basic medical kits they have prepared. Kits include medicines, nursing care items, and things like soap and toothbrushes. Sometimes they take food. Though on the trip the volunteers see beautiful scenery, inside the homes of those affected with HIV/AIDS the volunteers face serious illness. Sometimes unexpected things happen. Volunteers visited a teenaged girl who was in awful pain and had sores covering her face and body. The medicine the volunteers brought did not do much to relieve her pain so the volunteers prayed for comfort and healing. Two weeks later the volunteers returned expecting her to still be feeling badly. Instead they were greeted by this girl, her hair neatly braided, smiling at them and saying, "Jesus is healing me."

Prayer

God, you sent Jesus to teach and to heal. Today be with people who are sick or injured. Give them comfort and help them not to be afraid but to always remember you love them. Bless doctors, nurses, and caregivers. Give them strength so they can care for themselves and keep helping people. Amen.

What You Can Do

Ask your family to help you put together a health kit (or kits) that can be used by people in need in your community. In a ziplock plastic bag put several adhesive bandages, a travel-size bottle of antibacterial hand wash or a travel-size packet of wet wipes, a small squeeze tube of petroleum jelly, toothbrushes and a small tube of toothpaste, travel-size shampoo, and soap. You might think of other items to include. You can donate the health kits to homeless shelters or senior centers. Or see if your school can take them to give to children in need.

Did You Know?

Over 50 PC(USA) mission workers are involved in health ministries overseas. Many are doctors or nurses, but some, like Cindy Easterday, work to train people who care for those who are sick.

Giving What You Have

By words and deeds your church family helps people who are healing. Put 50 cents into your church offering plate on Sunday for each health kit you make to give thanks for the healing that can take place when people care for others.

MISSION IN THE UNITED STATES

Presbytery of Eastern Virginia

Does your church have an organization called Presbyterian Women? Do you know what the women of this group do in your church? Chances are they are very involved with mission of some sort. The Presbyterian Women (PW) in the Presbytery of Eastern Virginia have done all sorts of mission projects over the years. They started a new project after they sponsored five women from the Presbyterian Community of Kinshasa in the Democratic Republic of the Congo to visit eastern Virginia. People in the Presbytery of Eastern Virginia opened their homes to the women from Kinshasa for a week. The women of both countries got to be friends and listened to each other. The women from Kinshasa told the women of Virginia about orphans and other children in Kinshasa who didn't have enough to eat. After the women from Kinshasa went back home, the PW of the Presbytery of Eastern Virginia got money to start a feeding program for the orphans and other hungry

Scripture

Peter said to him, "Lord, you know everything; you know that I love you." Jesus said to him, "Feed my sheep" (John 21:17).

children in Kinshasa. Four feeding stations were set up. Now more than 400 children are fed one good meal each day. The women of the Presbytery of Eastern Virginia have listened to the words of Jesus when he said, "Feed my sheep." Find this presbytery on the map on page 112.

Presbyterian Women helped establish a feeding program for children in Kinshasa.

Puzzle: Listen to the Shepherd

Like a sheep, follow the instructions of the shepherd to find a message.

X P L Q F R D E N M P E C T D U J M G Z S Y
B O H J K S I L A H I E Z E U N P V K B F T R

- Cross out all of the following letters: X, V, B, R.

- Cross out the first and last letters of the alphabet.

- Cross out the letters in the word QUIT.

- Cross out the letters in the word KNOCK.

- Cross out all of the following letters: L, J, G.

- Cross out the 2nd, 7th, 10th, 11th, 21st, 25th, and 43rd letters in the lines of letters.

Answer: Feed my sheep

MISSION AROUND THE WORLD

Malawi

Charlotte Gott can remember the exact moment she felt called by God into mission service. Her church had invited Dr. Sue Makin, a mission co-worker in Malawi, to speak. The last picture Dr. Makin showed at her presentation was of a young Malawian boy holding a baby. Dr. Makin said, "Don't look at these children with American eyes. Look at them with God's eyes, because God has a purpose for them too." At that moment, Charlotte knew she wanted to do mission service.

Charlotte was appointed by the Church of Central Africa Presbyterian in 2004 to serve at Mulanje Mission Hospital in Malawi. After she arrived in Malawi and settled into her new home, she sat down to read her daily devotional. The Scripture for the day was John 21:17, where Jesus asks Peter to "feed my sheep." Charlotte wrestled with how to answer Jesus' call "to feed my sheep" in a land where most people don't live to be very old, where a lot of people are poor, and many are very sick. Dr. Makin's words that God had a purpose for the people of Malawi were comforting and gave Charlotte strength.

Charlotte writes, "Here in Malawi, my neighbors have no nice houses or fine cars or good clothes to hide behind. Their daily struggles and their suffering are all too visible to me as I drive past them or sit with them. They are the lame, the beggars, the mentally ill, those living and dying with AIDS, the starving, and the poor all around me. I see Christ walking with them. He looks no different than they do. 'Feed my sheep,' he begs me. And so I try."

Prayer

God of all people, you have taught us to feed your sheep, to love and care for all your people, especially the ones in need. Help me, like the people in the stories this week, to listen to other people. Help me to see even the small ways I can care for the people that you love. In Jesus' name. Amen.

What You Can Do

Pick up the phone and call someone! Choose a person whom you haven't spoken to for a while like a grandparent, relative, or friend, or a person you know does not get many visitors during the day. Remember to ask the person how he or she is doing. Let the person know you were thinking about them and that you care about them.

Giving What You Have

The Presbyterian Hunger Program offers an easy way for you to give to help people who are hungry. It's called Cents-Ability and is what used to be called Two-Cents-a-Meal, a program started by the Presbyterian Women. Now the Hunger Program suggests you and your family save 5 cents for each meal you eat. Find out more at the Hunger Program's Web site: www.pcusa.org/pcusa/wmd/hunger.

Word of the Week Hunger

Hunger is what you feel when your body needs food. Hunger can also be a longing for something besides food. When Jesus told us to feed his sheep, he meant more than making sure hungry people had food. What do you think he meant?

Did You Know?

Though we think of sheep as being farm animals, there are still wild sheep. Wild sheep called Argali are found in the mountains of Siberia and Mongolia. Wild sheep are excellent climbers.

MISSION IN THE UNITED STATES

Missouri Union Presbytery

Do you know how your church got started? If you don't know, ask your pastor or a long-time member to tell you the story. In Missouri, many Presbyterians trace their roots of faith to the Cumberland Presbyterian Church. These churches have always had traditional Reformed ways of worship. As new people move into the Missouri Union Presbytery and bring with them their traditions, Presbyterians find themselves reforming again. Worship in several churches in the central part of Missouri Union Presbytery has begun to change. Their worship experience is being enriched as more Spanish-speaking people join churches. Congregations are using the language and culture of these new members!

The presbytery recently heard the gospel preached in Hungarian as it celebrated its twentieth year of partnership with the Reformed Church in Hungary. At the celebration the presbytery committed to another partnership with the Reformed Church in Trans-Carpathian Ukraine. The partnership will offer the chance for churches in Missouri to share ideas, support, and prayers with churches in Hungary and Ukraine.

Isten hozott! Welcome! Bienvenido!

Word of the Week Reformed

The Presbyterian Church is part of the Reformed tradition. To reform means to make better. The Reformed tradition refers to the changes John Calvin and others made in some of the religious practices in the 1500s. New churches were started that used these changes, or reforms. Many of these churches around the world use the word Reformed in their name.

Scripture

How very good and pleasant it is when kindred live together in unity! (Psalm 133:1).

Craft

Soap Carving

Kenya is known for beautiful carved figures of wood and soapstone. The carvings range from people or African animals to abstract figures. Create your own sculpture out of soap!

Materials

a bath-sized bar of soft soap like Ivory
craft sticks
newspaper
pencil

Trace the shape of the bar of soap on paper to use as a guide. Draw an animal like a giraffe or elephant to fill the guide. Tape this drawing on the bar of soap and trace over the lines, pressing firmly to leave a groove in the soap. Before you start carving, spread newspaper out to catch the soap shavings. Use the craft stick like a knife to whittle away the outside areas of the figure. Remember to keep the soap shavings off of the floor. They are slippery! Don't try to whack off too large a piece at a time or you may break your soap. Leave one flat edge of the soap for a base. When the animal is finished, use a pencil to add details like eyes, ears, and mouth. Like Mr. Choi, leave a reminder of Jesus' love by carving a small cross in the bottom of the sculpture.

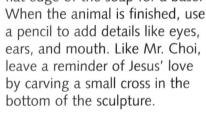

Giving What You Have

One of the things Mr. Choi does is teach. He helps people learn how to use their new prosthetic arms or legs. What skill do you have that you are really grateful for? Who taught that skill to you? Say thanks to that person.

Did You Know?

A Kenyan woman, Wangari Maathai, won the 2004 Nobel Peace Prize. The first African woman to be awarded the prize, she is known for her work to protect the environment and human rights. In the 1970s she started an effort, called the Green Belt Movement, to plant millions of trees across Africa.

What You Can Do

Check with your pastor to see if your presbytery is in partnership. Find out what activities are shared and how you can help.

Did You Know?

The Missouri Union Presbytery has a partnership with both the Reformed Church in Hungary and the Reformed Church in the Trans-Carpathian Ukraine. But did you know that Hungary and Ukraine also have a sort of partnership? They share a border in the Carpathian Mountains that is about 70 miles long.

Prayer

Dear God, be with people who have lost arms, legs, hands, or feet to accidents and acts of war. Bless all who help them regain abilities with prosthetic legs and arms and physical therapy. Fill our hearts with the wonder and wholeness of your creation when we look at ourselves and others. Amen.

MISSION AROUND THE WORLD

Kenya

Drs. Stan and Mia Topple are medical doctors serving as PC(USA) long-term volunteers in Kenya. Before working in Kenya, the Topples worked in Korea, where they met Seo Dong Choi. Mr. Choi had been a carpenter but learned how to make prosthetic (this means artificial) arms and legs for people who had lost limbs because of disease or accidents. After the Topples had worked in Kenya a while, Mr. Choi visited them. Because the need was great for someone with his skills, he moved to Kenya and helped people there who needed prosthetic arms and legs.

Mr. Choi visited a neighboring country, Somalia, where war had caused many people to be injured and lose arms and legs. He made several trips to Somalia after that to help the people who had been injured. He didn't speak the language of the Somalians, and the law of the land forbid him to share about God's love, but Mr. Choi left a message for his patients by putting a cross on a hidden part of the prosthetic arms and legs he made with the words "Jesus loves you."

Mr. Choi flies to places that need his help making prosthetic limbs.

Scripture

Word of the Week — Thanks

When we are grateful for something someone has given us or done for us, we say "thanks." When we realize all that God has given us, we say a double "thanks."

Give thanks to the LORD, bless the LORD's name. For the LORD is good (Psalm 100:4b–5a).

MISSION IN THE UNITED STATES

Presbytery of Southern Kansas

Whether your church sits in the middle of a big city or out past fields and pastures in the country, it might be easy to forget that we in the PC(USA) are all connected. Churches are busy places trying to do many things and sometimes forget about other churches. It's important to keep in touch with other churches to share concerns, ideas, and reasons to be thankful.

In the Presbytery of Southern Kansas three very different churches stopped being busy long enough to realize their need for one another. Find this presbytery on the map on page 112. Covenant Presbyterian Church is made up of members who live in the city or suburbs; Brotherhood Presbyterian has mostly African American members; and Wichita Korean is a Korean Presbyterian congregation. The three churches all saw the benefit of working together. They decided to share an evening of giving thanks and praise. For the last three years the three congregations have shared a Thanksgiving meal and worship service the week before the Thanksgiving holiday. Leaders from all three churches take part in the service, and elements of each church's traditions are used in one joyous service to thank God for all their blessings.

Recipe
Fruit Salad

As the summer comes to an end, we in the United States usually have an abundance of fruits and vegetables still in season. Even though we celebrate Thanksgiving in November, why not have a summer thanksgiving feast that includes the plentiful foods of the season?

In a bowl combine the following:
2 peeled and diced peaches
10 strawberries cut in half
1 cup of blueberries, rinsed
2 peeled and sliced kiwi
cantaloupe or honeydew melon, sliced
seedless grapes cut in half

Stir in one 8-oz. cup of vanilla yogurt.
Squeeze in 1 tsp. of lemon juice.
Stir again. Serve as a dessert or a side dish.

MISSION AROUND THE WORLD

Lesotho

After spending two years in Lesotho, [pronounced luh-SUE-two] sometimes we forget that many of the things we see here daily would be considered unusual in North America," wrote Samantha Franklin, a former mission co-worker in Lesotho. "On my drive home I saw a small group of children each carrying a large bag of maize meal [cornmeal] to their home in a nearby village. A few minutes later I saw another group of four children loading water jugs into a wheelbarrow to be taken to their home nearby. In this part of the world, children's roles and responsibilities within the family are often so different than what we are used to seeing in North America."

Samantha volunteered once a week at Maseru Children's Village, a home for children. Each year a women's group in the area sponsors a Christmas party for the children and gives them gifts. In 2003 the highlight of the party came when the queen of Lesotho appeared. She greeted each child and presented him or her with a gift from the women's group that was sponsoring the party. The children were thrilled and thanked the queen by singing some songs for her.

Find Lesotho on the map on page 111. As you do, think about how your life is different from the lives of the children talked about in these stories.

Lesotho's Queen Masenate presents a Christmas gift at Maseru Children's Village.

Prayer

After doing a chore around the house, sit quietly and think about children your age who work daily and whose families could not survive without their work. Pray: *God, remember and bless children who work around the world. Keep them safe in dangerous jobs and keep them hopeful in dull tasks. Be with children who dream of a better life and give your church everywhere a dedication to helping such children. Amen.*

Lesotho is slightly smaller in area than Maryland. Look in the Mission Yearbook *for Prayer & Study on the page for Lesotho and find out how many languages are spoken there and how many people live there.*

Did You Know?

In Lesotho, you would say Merry Christmas like this: Keresemese ha monate.

Giving What You Have

Thankful words are a wonderful gift. Who are you most grateful for at this moment? You can call, write a note to, or visit that person to thank him or her for their special place in your life.

What You Can Do

Volunteer to do an extra chore around your home today—something that would truly help your household. Offer to do this extra chore for the week. Remember the many children in other countries who do chores that keep their homes going every day.

MISSION IN THE UNITED STATES

John Calvin Presbytery

Kansas, Missouri

In May 2003 tornadoes tore through areas of John Calvin Presbytery. (Find this presbytery on the map on page 112.) Homes, stores, buildings, and churches were destroyed. The worst damage was in Stockton, Missouri, where the Ross Memorial Presbyterian Church is. The church's roof blew completely off, walls were left barely standing, and the entire front of the sanctuary had dropped into the basement. The congregation's members gathered at the site of the church soon after the storm ended to see what damage had been done. What members saw made them sad because this building had been holy ground for them, and now it was destroyed. The elders and the pastor would not let the church family stay sad. They rescued what they could from the old church building and quickly found a place where the congregation could meet and worship. The Stockton Church of God welcomed them and allowed them to use its building to worship and have programs. Prayers and gifts came in from around the country. Presbyterian Disaster Relief answered prayers by sending funds. People from Stockton and nearby communities came out to help. In October a service was held near the destroyed building to celebrate the life of Ross Memorial Presbyterian Church and to start work on a new building. Thankful for all the support received from the presbytery, the PC(USA), and people from the community, the church was ready for a new beginning.

Did You Know?

Tornadoes are most likely to occur between 3:00 and 9:00 P.M. A tornado watch is when conditions are possible for a tornado in your area. A tornado warning is when a tornado has been seen in your area.

Scripture

God called to Moses out of the bush, "Moses, Moses!" And he said, "Here I am." Then God said, "Come no closer! Remove the sandals from your feet, for the place on which you are standing is holy ground" (Exodus 3:4–5).

Ross Memorial Presbyterian Church rises again after suffering damage from a tornado.

Puzzle: Find Holy

How many times can you find the word HOLY? You may go up, down, forward, backward, or diagonally. See if you can find it 10 times.

```
Z M O H O L Y G E W I O
H U I O P F L J B H L W
O J S L X Q O A R O J Y
L W E Y P I H K S L B L
Y Y L O H U K M O Y M O
S O K H K D T S Y L O H
H O L Y K H G V S T W Q
```

MISSION AROUND THE WORLD

Rwanda

Have you ever been someplace and felt that God was present? Maybe you have stepped into a beautiful church or a forest and felt you were in a sacred space. Moses stood on desert ground and heard God's voice tell him it was a holy place. It may have just been an ordinary place to other people, but God was letting Moses know that God was present right there. In Rwanda, it may be hard to walk into a building where a tragedy occurred and feel that it is a holy place. But a religious college in Rwanda that is a partner of the PC(USA) is a place where God is present. In 1994 there was a war between two groups of people in Rwanda. Many buildings in the country were damaged and people were injured or killed. During that war some of the people at the college were killed and the buildings damaged. The college closed its doors in April 1994 and did not open again until October 1995. Since then several denominations including Presbyterians have joined together to bring teachers and students back to the college. People in the community have again begun to see the college as a place where God is present and not just one of the places in the country where tragedy happened. With prayers and God's guidance the college is again training young people to be ministers who will serve in Rwanda. Find this country on the map on pages 110–111.

Students at a religious college in Rwanda train for the future.

Prayer

Sit quietly someplace and think about a time that you have felt God was nearby or present with you. Perhaps you felt this holiness at a summer camp, a special worship service, or the birth or death of someone in your family. Thinking of that event, remember how you thought and felt. Pray: *God of life, thank you for those moments when you are so near that I can feel your presence. Teach me to know and believe that I can always seek you out when I feel alone. Amen.*

Giving What You Have

On October 2 many churches in the PC(USA) will receive the Peacemaking Offering. The offering's money will go for projects that promote peace in your community, in your presbytery, and across the PC(USA). For the next few weeks you can save money to give to the offering. This week, set aside 25 cents for each time it rains.

What You Can Do

Ask your church school teacher if your class can organize a way to help people who have experienced a tornado. Assemble Clean-up Buckets. These kits provide the basic tools people need to clean up after a disaster. The directions are on the Presbyterian Disaster Assistance Web site: www.pcusa.org/pda/help/cleanup-kit.htm.

Word of the Week Holy

When something is holy, it is seen as sacred and you can feel that God is present. It belongs to God or comes from God. In this week's Scripture verse, Moses felt God's presence on the ground where he was standing.

MISSION IN THE UNITED STATES

Presbytery of the Mid-South

Tennessee, Arkansas, Missouri

Have you ever thought of mission work as being fun? The children at Idlewild Presbyterian Church, in Memphis, Tennessee, think so. Not only is mission work fun at Idlewild but it is creative too. On Wednesday evenings two groups meet at Idlewild to learn about the needs of God's people and find out ways to be kind to them. The Small Samaritans and Micah's Missionaries are in first through sixth grade. The Small Samaritans take their name from the story Jesus told about the good Samaritan (see Luke 10:30–37). Micah's Missionaries are named after the prophet who wrote the book of Micah. The Scripture verse for this week is a verse that inspires them.

The two groups have had several projects. They have shined the shoes of church members after worship services to raise money for children in Afghanistan. They have collected diapers for a local HIV/AIDS day-care center. They have baked cookies and made valentines for a children's homeless shelter and sold Christmas cards using their own artwork to buy food for a local food pantry that helps people needing food. Mission has a new face in Memphis—it is young, kind, playful, and giggly. Through the joyful service of these students, mission in Memphis is cool!

Idlewild Presbyterian Church is a part of the Presbytery of the Mid-South. Find this presbytery on the map on page 112.

Children at Idlewild Presbyterian Church helped buy food for a local food pantry.

Scripture

What does the LORD require of you but to do justice, and to love kindness, and to walk humbly with your God? (Micah 6:8).

Craft

Healing Rice Bags

Make a healing rice bag. When warmed, these bags can be placed around a sore neck or on another place that aches and can help those sore places feel better. Follow the instructions below for warming a bag once you have made one.

Materials

1 pound of brown rice
1 large adult male athletic sock or 1 small pillowcase (as for a baby pillow)
needle and thread

Fill about half the sock or pillowcase with rice. The sock or pillowcase should have plenty of rice in it, but it should also have lots of room to move around so you can make it fit around your neck or back. Thread a needle, and with small, close, and tight stitches, sew the top of the sock or pillowcase. Remember to sew from edge to edge so no rice can sneak out. When you have finished sewing, tie the thread in a knot. When you want to use your healing rice bag, place it in the center of a microwave and put it on two minutes (quite hot) or one minute and 30 seconds (medium warm). Take it out and place it on the area that is sore.

Giving What You Have

Remember to save money for the Peacemaking Offering. Put in 25 cents for each scoop of rice you eat this week. Ask your family to do the same.

MISSION AROUND THE WORLD

Liberia

Sometimes helping someone in need means giving something of one's own. That is what the Presbytery of Arkansas did. Its members gave 176,000 pounds of rice grown in Dewitt, Arkansas, to people in Liberia. The Presbyterian Disaster Assistance (PDA) team visited Liberia. The country was in ruins because of a very long war. Buildings were destroyed, fields could not grow crops, and people were hungry. The PDA team asked Presbyterians to help. In just five weeks, the Presbytery of Arkansas raised almost $15,000 so it could buy rice to send to Liberia. The rice was put on a ship in October 2003 and it arrived in December. From the harbor it was loaded onto five trucks, and churches and other helping organizations delivered the rice to the people. The Arkansas rice and the kindness that brought the rice to Liberia were joyfully received by all.

Prayer

Place several uncooked grains of rice in your hand. Feel the texture of the rice. Think about cooked rice, how it feels and looks when it is all fluffy and warm. Think about the millions of people today who will grow rice, cook rice, and eat rice. Holding the rice tightly in your hand, pray: *O God, be with those who are eating rice wherever they are in the world. Help them to have enough rice that they will not be hungry and bless them so that they may eat their rice in peace. In Jesus' name. Amen.*

Did You Know?

In Burma a person eats 500 pounds of rice a year, which is 1 1/4 pounds per day. The Chinese word for rice and food is the same. In Thailand when you call your family to a meal you say, "Eat rice."

Word of the Week
Kindness

Kindness is when somebody helps another person in a gentle and caring way so that you know the kind person wants what's best for the other.

What You Can Do

Think of an older person in your church or neighborhood who might enjoy the healing rice bag. Give it to that person and explain how to use it. Make sure he or she has a microwave oven!

MISSION IN THE UNITED STATES

Presbytery of Middle Tennessee

When a few people work together, lots of wonderful things can be done. When lots of people get together, an amazing difference can occur in the world. When the youth of Priest Lake Presbyterian Church first thought of developing a mission project, their aim was to help several youth groups from small churches manage a bigger project than any group could do alone. They started Project J.O.Y. (Joyous Offerings of Youth) and had 71 volunteers from 20 churches in the presbytery teaming up to help more than 1,000 people in need. The churches collected food, clothes, and gifts. The Presbyterian Hunger Program of the Presbytery of Middle Tennessee also gave money to J.O.Y. (Find this presbytery on the map on page 112.) After the youth gathered all the supplies to give away, they took them to the people in need.

They helped one family carry boxes of supplies and discovered that the family lived in a car. The youth were speechless. When they got home they talked about all the nice things they owned and took for granted. They decided to be more aware of the difference a small amount of money makes when you have nothing, not even basic shelter or food.

Word of the Week Interfaith

Interfaith refers to something that happens between two or more religions. Sometimes we have interfaith services, which means people of different faiths or religions, like Christians, Jews, and Muslims, have a service that focuses on what they have in common.

Scripture

The LORD is gracious and merciful. . . . The LORD is good to all (Psalm 145:8–9).

Recipe

Fried Yams

Make sure you have an adult to help you as you make this recipe.

Ingredients

2 large yams
vegetable oil
salt

Peel and slice yams in pieces about 1/2 inch thick. Put vegetable oil in a skillet on low heat. Oil should be about 3/4 inch high so it will cover a yam slice. Place yam slices in heated oil. Cook until brown, then turn the slices and brown the other side. Remove from skillet and put on a plate lined with a paper towel. Salt to taste.

Did You Know?

In Nigeria 4,000 different dialects are spoken.

MISSION AROUND THE WORLD

Nigeria

"If we cannot live together, why do we claim to be worshiping God?" asked Nigeria's president, Olusegun Obasanjo. Obasanjo is a Christian. He recognizes that there are deep divisions between the Christian and Muslim communities in his country. But the president, along with Christian and Muslim leaders, is calling for members of both faiths to get along and not hurt each other.

With over 126 million people in the country, Nigeria probably has more Christians and Muslims living side by side than any other nation. In recent years more tension and violence have occurred between the two faith communities.

The Project for Christian-Muslim Relations in Africa has had an important but difficult job. The project has tried to help Christians and Muslims have a better understanding of one another. It has brought Christians and Muslims together to discuss what the two faiths have in common and what differences there are. Not only have they had interfaith discussions; they have also worked on projects together in the community. The president and religious leaders hope interfaith discussions and projects will help the people live in peace.

Friday Inya is a pastor helping Muslims and Christians understand each other.

Prayer

Think about someone you know or even someone you don't know who belongs to a different faith. Think about how God would want you to pray for that person. Pray: *God of all the world, be with people of every faith. Hear the prayers of all the people who talk to you. Help me so that I never use the differences in belief and faith as an excuse to think less of someone or feel that I am better than them. Amen.*

Look at the art on the cover of the Mission Yearbook for Prayer & Study and compare it to the art on the cover of your Children's Yearbook. How are they alike? How are they different? Was one cover the inspiration for the other one?

Giving What You Have

For each time you play a favorite game, save 10 cents for the Peacemaking Offering.

What You Can Do

Do you know someone who belongs to a different faith? Find out something about that faith. Think about what things your faith and your friend's faith share. Do they both worship God? If you feel close enough to the person of the other faith, ask him or her questions about the religion. Avoid arguing about your faiths.

MISSION IN THE UNITED STATES
Presbytery of Mid-Kentucky

The skinny 11-year-old girl from Louisville's West End tugged at a carrot top on a sunny morning in June. Other children around the garden plot strained over their carrots, trying not to trample the tomato seedlings planted nearby. For most of these children this was the first time they had gotten food from the earth rather than a grocery store. The carrot finally came flying up from the ground. Rinsing off her carrot prize, the little girl took a bite. Yum! She grinned and took another big bite. "Mr. Stephen, this is good," she said. "This is the first time I have ever eaten a carrot."

Thus ended the first week of Gardening Day Camp at the John Leake Memorial Garden behind Crescent Hill Presbyterian Church in Louisville, Kentucky. This church is in the Presbytery of Mid-Kentucky. Find this presbytery on the map on page 112. For a week at a time groups of children

Scripture

The LORD sets the prisoners free; the LORD opens the eyes of the blind. The LORD lifts up those who are bowed down; the LORD loves the righteous (Psalm 146:7b–8).

ranging from six to 14 years of age spent their days doing gardening chores, picking blueberries and raspberries, slurping watermelon, grinding corn by hand, canning hot salsa, and having lessons about food and taking care of the earth. Toward the end of the afternoon they walked to the public pool for a cool swim. What truly fascinated the children about this garden was that it was open to anyone who wanted to get food from there. Any hungry person could go to the garden at any time and take food for free. It was a taste of freedom and an end to fences and "keep out" signs to the children.

Puzzle: Changing Times

Find the six things that have changed from the first picture to the next.

Answers: 1. No curtains in window. 2. Different flower in windowbox. 3. Leaf is missing.
4. Large rock instead of 2 small rocks. 5. Inner tube is different. 6. Cat has no claws.

Stephen Bartlett

Children and a camp counselor grind corn for a batch of cornbread at the John Leake Memorial Garden at Crescent Hill Presbyterian Church in Louisville.

MISSION AROUND THE WORLD

Niger

If you go to Niger (pronounced NIGH-jur, or NEE-zher), you might get to ride a camel! That's because so much of the land is desert. In fact, 80 percent of the land is in the Sahara Desert. The PC(USA)'s partner church in Niger is the Evangelical Church of Niger. It runs a Bible school called Dogon Gao (pronounced DOH gun gow) with about 30 students who are learning to be ministers. These students get to study all the things that people who are going to be ministers usually study; but they also get training in how to do other kinds of work that will help them make enough money to support their families. Niger is a poor country, and most of the churches in Niger can't afford to support a pastor. So the pastors have other jobs to make money. When a pastor or mission worker has another job besides being pastor, it's called tentmaking.

Tom Johnson is a PC(USA) development worker who works with the Evangelical Church of Niger and its Bible school. One of his jobs is to help the students and the school develop some jobs and projects that make money so the school can keep going and the students can keep studying. The school has lots of land around it, so Tom has decided to get the school some goats. By selling milk from the goats, the school can earn money. Students can be taught how to take care of goats and be paid for their work. So now Tom is raising money to buy the goats. Find Niger on the map on pages 110–111.

Prayer

Dear God, thank you for all the wonderful vegetables, fruits, and berries you have planted on your earth to feed us. Bless the children of the Gardening Day Camp as they learn about growing food. And bless the students at Dogon Gao in Niger as they study. Amen.

What You Can Do

Find out if there is a public garden in your community and how it works. Would you like to garden? Maybe there is a fall vegetable you could grow in a small corner of your yard or in the public garden. When the vegetable is ripe and ready to be picked, give some to a family in need or to your neighbors.

Did You Know?

Native American Day is September 22 this year. In 1994 the 206th General Assembly approved this day to teach Presbyterians about Native ministries and to learn about Native people.

Word of the Week   Tentmaker

A tentmaker is a minister or mission worker who also works at another job to earn a living. It's called tentmaking because the apostle Paul made tents for a living while he was a missionary (Acts 18:1–3).

Giving What You Have

Make a list of all the vegetables you and your family enjoy eating. Now put aside 10 cents for the Peacemaking Offering for each one named.

MISSION IN THE UNITED STATES

Midwest Hanmi Presbytery

Nongeographic

If you look at the map of the United States on page 112, you will see the groups of states that make up the 16 synods in the PC(USA). Find the Synod of Lincoln Trails. (Hint: Look for the states of Illinois and Indiana.) You'll see the different presbyteries that make up the synod, and you will see an arrow reaching from the top of the synod up to the name Midwest Hanmi. It's called a nongeographic presbytery because, unlike the other presbyteries, it's not formed by churches in a particular area but by Korean American churches that might be anywhere in the United States. The word Hanmi means "Korea-America."

The Presbyterians in Midwest Hanmi have a new project: they are reaching out to people from Mongolia who have moved to Chicago. Find Mongolia just above China on the map on page 111. Mongolian people have been coming to the United States to go to school, to get job training in new technology, and to learn how to manage businesses. Korean American Presbyterians are helping them in these areas as well as telling them about God's love for them. Hanmee Presbyterian Church, which is located in one of Chicago's suburbs, is supporting a Korean mission pastor who can speak in both Mongolian and Korean languages.

Did You Know?

Within the PC(USA) are five nongeographic presbyteries. You may remember from the story about Midwest Hanmi Presbytery that nongeographic means the presbytery is not formed by churches within a certain geographic area like other presbyteries are, but is formed by churches that could be anywhere in the United States. Four of them are Korean American presbyteries and one is a Native American presbytery.

Scripture

Let the same mind be in you that was in Christ Jesus (Philippians 2:5).

Craft

Batik

While the weather is still nice, try this outside project inspired by the beautiful cloth made in Africa. (You might need to ask for help from an adult or older sibling.)

Materials

a white cotton T-shirt or white cotton handkerchief
cardboard
white glue
paper cup or margarine tub
several colors of cold water dye
paint brushes of various sizes
spray bottles or buckets (same number needed as number of colors of dye)

※ Outside in a grassy area that can't be harmed or ruined by a little permanent dye, set up spray bottles or buckets of the cold water dye. Follow the instructions on the package to mix the dye.

※ Put a piece of cardboard inside the T-shirt or pin the handkerchief onto a piece of cardboard.

※ Pour white glue into a paper cup or an empty margarine tub. Using the paint brushes and glue, paint a design on the front of the cloth. Make sure the glue coat is thick.

※ If you want to repeat the process on the other side of the T-shirt, make sure the glue is dry before you turn the shirt over and repeat the process. (You cannot use both sides of a thin cotton cloth like a handkerchief.)

※ When the glue is completely dried, spray paint colors over the design. Or dip the cloth into the buckets halfway and then switch buckets and dip the cloth's other side in a new color.

※ Let dry overnight.

※ Rinse in cold water to remove the glue. Some dye will also rinse off at this time. Wash the cloth in hot water to set the color. Let the shirt or cloth air dry.

Giving What You Have

Do you remember how many nongeographic presbyteries there are in the PC(USA)? (The answer is somewhere in this week's pages.) For each nongeographic presbytery, save 25 cents to put in the Peacemaking Offering on October 2.

The church is working to give Congolese youth a future full of hope.

Word of the Week Cooperation

Cooperation is working together for a common purpose. Who is cooperating in the story about the Democratic Republic of the Congo? Who in the Midwest Hanmi Presbytery story?

What You Can Do

Has your church signed the Commitment to Peacemaking? This commitment says that your church will include peacemaking efforts in its ministry and mission. Since next week is when most PC(USA) churches receive the Peacemaking Offering, now is a good time to get your church to sign the commitment. Ask your church school teacher or your pastor about the commitment. You can find it on the PC(USA)'s Web site at www.pcusa.org/peacemaking/commitment.htm. The commitment is one way you and your church can work toward peace in places like the Democratic Republic of the Congo.

Prayer

Dear God, bless the Korean American Presbyterians in their work with Mongolian people living in the United States. Bless also the people of the Congo and the churches cooperating to make health care better there. Amen.

MISSION AROUND THE WORLD

Democratic Republic of the Congo

A five-year civil war has left 3.5 million people dead in the Democratic Republic of the Congo. The economy has also been destroyed. An average family lives on $89 for a whole year. But within the last year the people of the Congo have had reason to hope for a better life. A new government with representation from each of the warring rebel groups has helped these groups stop fighting and unite to strengthen the country. During the war and now in its aftermath, the PC(USA), along with other denominations, has played a major role in meeting the people's basic needs for food, shelter, health care, and spiritual nurture. The PC(USA), other Protestant churches, and the Catholic Church are involved in the largest church-run health program. This program attempts to serve a population of 12 million people. Health centers distribute vaccines, medicine, and education to the Congolese people. What these health centers teach is as important as the medicine and medical care they can offer. Classes that help the people understand what they can do to prevent illnesses and the spread of disease are offered, as is basic first aid. The people of the Congo and the churches working in partnership with them are striving to follow in the healing steps of Jesus Christ. Find this country on the map on page 111.

Peacemaking Offering

MISSION IN THE UNITED STATES
Presbytery of Detroit
Michigan

It was a very special kind of class reunion. Gratiot Avenue Presbyterian Church and First Presbyterian Church of Brighton sponsored an event called "Better Together" at the Martin Luther King High School in Detroit. The event celebrated the fiftieth anniversary of an important Supreme Court decision known as Brown versus the Board of Education. It stated that all students, regardless of race and color, should have equal access to the same schools. Making the journey to Detroit for the celebration were Elizabeth Eckford and Kendal Reinhardt. Ms. Eckford had been one of the nine black students who first integrated Central High School in Little Rock, Arkansas. It is hard to imagine today what that must have been like. On September 2, 1957, Ms. Eckford's family prepared her for her first day of school. She was met at the front steps of the school by an angry mob, threatening to physically

Scripture

Guide our feet into the way of peace
(Luke 1:79)

harm and possibly kill her. Eventually, the President of the United States ordered the National Guard to protect and assist the nine black students to safely enter the school. What courageous steps those children took as they approached their new school.

Entering the school was only the first step. Ms. Eckford and the others were subject to insults and violence. A few students offered them welcome and friendship. Among those students who welcomed Ms. Eckford was Mr. Reinhardt. The reunion in Detroit celebrated the long and difficult path to end racial injustice. Participants renewed their commitments to build schools, churches, and a society where justice is done and all are welcomed and treated as people created in the image of God.

Craft
Peace Box
Materials

shoebox
magazines and/or personal photos
nature items like stones, leaves,
    objects that attract you
newspapers
paper
pen or pencil
scissors
glue

Cover a shoebox by gluing words and pictures cut from magazines or personal photos and images that depict God's peace at work in the world. You can fill the box with news clippings, notes, photos, and items from nature that inspire you to live in the way of peace.

MISSION AROUND THE WORLD

Sudan

In Sudan millions of people have been walking to find peace. Most of them are refugees who have been fleeing their homes and villages, looking for safe places to live and enough food to eat. A civil war lasting more than 35 years has pitted the Sudanese government against the people in southern Sudan and, more recently, against people in western Sudan. The government has destroyed whole villages along with their crops and cattle so that their food sources are gone.

Some of the Sudanese people walking to find peace have been on their way to one of several peace conferences, where they are trying to work out problems with each other. Even though their main enemy has been the government, the different tribes of the south have been fighting one another also. With the help of the New Sudan Council of Churches (NSCC) and the Presbyterian Church of Sudan, both partners of the PC(USA) that work with people in southern Sudan, people of different tribes have met and discussed their differences, bringing more peace to their land. PC(USA) mission co-worker Haruun Ruun, the executive secretary of NSCC, has been pleased with the peace conferences and now is hopeful about the peace work between southern Sudan and the government. It is his prayer that all the people of Sudan can walk in peace.

New Sudan Council of Churches, courtesy of Church World Service

Sudanese youth walk to a peace talk.

Word of the Week Journey

When we take a journey, we go from one place to another. Refugees go from their homes to a place they often don't know but believe is safer than their homes. Elizabeth Eckford made a journey to a new school after the Brown versus the Board of Education decision in 1954 and helped the country make a journey toward integration. Whenever we take a journey, we can ask God to help us travel in the way of peace.

What You Can Do

If your church is receiving the Peacemaking Offering, how is it planning to spend its 25 percent of the offering? If the church is doing something that you can help with, volunteer to help. Or learn more about the Presbyterian Peacemaking Program at www.pcusa.org/peacemaking. This year it celebrates its twenty-fifth anniversary.

Did You Know?

The Peacemaking Offering is one of four special offerings of the PC(USA). It's usually received on the first Sunday in October, which is also World Communion Sunday. After the offering is received, churches will keep 25 percent of what is received to help them practice peacemaking in their own communities.

Giving What You Have

Count the number of shoes in your home. For each shoe give a penny to the Peacemaking Offering.

Prayer

God of peace, help us to walk in the ways of peace. In Christ's name. Amen.

MISSION IN THE UNITED STATES

Presbytery of Blackhawk

Illinois

Church-related camp and conference ministries offer places and times for God's children of all ages to "get away from it all" and relax in God's presence. The leaders at Stronghold Conference, Retreat and Camping Center near Oregon, Illinois, recognize the meaningful experiences people have while at camp. Stronghold began several programs for groups that usually wouldn't be attending a church camp. "Stronghold Challenges" is one such program designed for young people and adults who want to understand themselves better and want to learn how to work and live with others better. The challenges take place on a high ropes course, in the heart of the woods, and through games around the camp property. People in the program learn skills that help them succeed in school, at work, and in their personal lives. In another program the camp works with an educational organization for people convicted of driving under the influence of drugs or alcohol. Stronghold also uses its lovely environment to help elementary school students from the area learn more about math, science, language, and the fine arts.

By inviting groups who might not normally be in that setting to use the camp, Stronghold is opening the door to helping others feel God's presence in their lives. Stronghold Center is in the Presbytery of Blackhawk. Find this presbytery on the map on page 112.

Word of the Week   Mission

Mission is about letting others know of God's love for all people shown us through Jesus. Sometimes we do this in words, sometimes in our actions. Sometimes we do it one by one. Sometimes we do it in partnership with other people, like the PC(USA) does with the Presbyterian Church of Ghana.

Scripture

If I speak in the tongues of mortals and of angels, but do not have love, I am a noisy gong or a clanging cymbal (1 Corinthians 13:1).

Craft

Adinkra "Cloth" Place Mats

Remember what the sankofa bird was doing in the story about Ghana this week? The sankofa is an Adinkra (ah-DEEN-krah) symbol. Adinkra cloths are hand-printed patterned cloths that tell stories through symbols. You can make your own Adinkra "cloth" into place mats.

Directions

Draw a few of the Adinkra symbols below on craft foam sheets (available at craft stores) or sponges and cut them out. With an adult's help, hot glue each symbol to a piece of cardboard. Holding the cardboard end, dip the symbol into a shallow pan with black tempera paint. Stamp the symbols in patterns on an 11 x 17" sheet of copy paper and let dry.

 Adinkrahene
greatness, charisma, leadership

 Nyame Biribi Wo Soro
hope

 Bi Nka Bi
peace, harmony

 Sankofa (alternate)
learn from the past

 Ese Ne Tekrema
friendship, sharing

 Dwennimmen
humility and strength

 Akoma
patience & tolerance

MISSION AROUND THE WORLD

Ghana

A popular image in western Africa is the sankofa bird shown reaching back over its shoulder to retrieve an egg. The egg is a symbol of the bird's own beginning. The bird is reaching back to "catch sight" of where it began. This image is also a symbol for how African Christians are reaching back to reclaim a Christian identity that is rooted in their own soil, back at their very beginning.

One place where African Christians can do this "reaching back" is at the Akrofi-Christaller Memorial Centre for Mission Research and Applied Theology (ACC). The center was established by the Presbyterian Church of Ghana, which is a PC(USA) partner. It is a place where Christian pastors can gain the education they need to be more effective in leading the church's mission. As a Presbyterian institution, ACC remains faithful in its studies and teaching methods to the Reformed tradition. Like students at other seminaries, students at ACC must take traditional classes in the Old and New Testaments, Reformed theology, Christian history, and preaching. These students are also trained to record local history and to understand people's faith within their experiences. As the students of ACC encourage people to share their experiences and their tradition, they can see people being transformed. The people become like the sankofa bird. They begin to find their roots in a loving and caring God. Find Ghana on the map on page 110.

The sankofa bird serves as a symbol for us to learn from the past.

Prayer

God, you love me and know me. Please come near to me as I pray that I will always have a sense of a mission to do in faithfulness to you. I believe now that my mission is to . . . (name what you think your mission is). As I strive to do this mission, please give me the gifts I need to do it well. In Jesus' name. Amen.

Giving What You Have

Help stop hunger in your community and around the world by putting 5 cents for each meal you eat in a jar and bringing it to your church next Sunday. The Presbyterian Hunger Program's Cents-Ability raises thousands of dollars each year to fight hunger just by asking people like you to contribute 5 cents a meal.

Look in the 2005 Mission Yearbook for Prayer & Study *on page 277 and see if you can find out how old the Presbyterian Peacemaking Program is this year. It is something to celebrate!*

Did You Know?

In our nation's capital, Washington D.C., one in three children does not get enough food to eat and is poorly nourished. In the United States one in five children is living in poverty.

What You Can Do

World Food Day is October 16. This annual event is observed worldwide to highlight hunger and hunger-related problems around the world. Find out more by viewing the Presbyterian Hunger Program's Web page at www.pcusa.org/pcusa/wmd/hunger. If your church or community is having a Hunger Walk, ask your parents or caregiver if you can join the walk.

Scripture

Let the peoples praise you, O God; let all the peoples praise you (Psalm 67:3).

Neema men sing as the Neema Fellowship celebrates with First Church in Mishawaka.

MISSION IN THE UNITED STATES

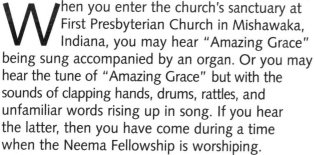

Presbytery of Wabash Valley

Indiana

When you enter the church's sanctuary at First Presbyterian Church in Mishawaka, Indiana, you may hear "Amazing Grace" being sung accompanied by an organ. Or you may hear the tune of "Amazing Grace" but with the sounds of clapping hands, drums, rattles, and unfamiliar words rising up in song. If you hear the latter, then you have come during a time when the Neema Fellowship is worshiping.

The Neema Fellowship is made up of immigrants from Kenya. Go to the world map on page 111 and find Kenya in eastern Africa. The immigrants in the Neema Fellowship are a long way from their home country. Members of the Neema Fellowship worship with language, music, and traditions from their culture and share in celebrations with their host congregation. Although language and certain customs are different for the two congregations, the desire to praise God is a common bond that unites them. Together the leaders of the Mishawaka church and the Neema Fellowship explore ways to meet the spiritual and material needs of the members of both congregations.

First Presbyterian Church of Mishawaka is in the Presbytery of Wabash Valley. Find this presbytery on the map on page 112.

Craft

Illustrated Hymns

For children who don't yet read, looking at a hymn in the hymnal is like looking at a foreign language. Pictures can help them connect meanings with words. Make an illustrated hymnbook for a child who doesn't yet read.

Choose your favorite hymn, a hymn that will be used next Sunday, or "Amazing Grace," #280 in *The Presbyterian Hymnal*.

You'll need markers, a hymnal, cardstock paper or old file folders cut in half and trimmed to make pages, scissors, old magazines, and glue.

* Read through the hymn. What images come to mind when you read the words?
* Go through the magazines and find pictures that closely resemble the images you thought of when you read the hymn.
* On one side of an old file folder or cardstock paper print clearly and boldly the name of the hymn and its number.
* On the other side of the paper, print the first line of the hymn, using about one-inch letters. Then choose a magazine picture that illustrates this line. Draw your own pictures if you can't find one in a magazine.
* Go through each line of the hymn, writing it in large print and finding a picture to illustrate its meaning. Use the front and back of as many pieces of cardstock as you need to do the first verse.
* Gather the pages like a book and staple together at the top and bottom of the left side. Now you have a hymnbook!

MISSION AROUND THE WORLD

Cameroon

Imagine if in your church you were to worship each Sunday in a language other than your native language. Would you feel left out at times? Even if you enjoyed the songs' rhythms and melodies, you might get frustrated by not being able to join in the singing or understand what was being sung. So, it isn't surprising that the new Hallelujah Choir in the Presbyterian Church in Cameroon is so popular with people. (Find Cameroon on the map on page 110.)

Unlike other choirs in churches in this area of Africa that use more westernized, traditional church music, the Hallelujah Choir uses only traditional instruments and sings in local languages. Their songs are new songs proclaiming the faith of a new generation. Talented musicians and singers share their gifts of music in ways that were not encouraged before. People in the communities are hearing the traditional music and being moved by the new words of a strong faith. Smiles appear on faces in the congregation as the choir begins to sing. The new songs are weaving the people's faith together with their roots and culture.

What You Can Do

Get some friends together to make illustrated hymns using the instructions for this week's craft. After you have made several hymns, give them to your church's preschool or kindergarten class.

Did You Know?

Mount Cameroon is the highest mountain in West Africa and is an active volcano! The local people call Mount Cameroon the "chariot of the Gods." It has erupted six times in the last 100 years. Each year there is a race up to the top of the mountain and a great celebration for the winners.

Word of the Week — Hallelujah

Hallelujah means "praise the Lord." This is not a word to say or sing with a frown on your face!

The Hallelujah Choir sings songs of praise to God in their native language.

Giving What You Have

Give your time! Call a family in your church or someone on your block who has a preschool child and offer to read to or play with their child for an hour. The attention from an older person like yourself will probably be welcomed by a younger child and the child's parent.

Prayer

Hallelujah is often shouted or sung in Christian communities around the world especially when they think of the great things God has done. People singing or shouting Hallelujah are often experiencing joy they feel in that moment. Think about the things that God has done in your life that give you joy. As you think of each of these joys say "hallelujah!" Amen.

MISSION IN THE UNITED STATES

Presbytery of Minnesota Valleys

Minnesota, South Dakota

The Dakota, Cheyenne, and for a time the Iowa tribes populated the area of southwestern Minnesota. Then came the immigrants from Scandinavian countries who were moving west to find land they could farm. Today, rural Minnesota is continuing to welcome new people. The new immigrants aren't used to the cold winters or whipping wind. These immigrants are from Sudan, the largest country in Africa. As we learned the week of October 2–8 (pages 84–85), millions of Sudanese have left their homes because of civil war. Many of these refugees have moved to the United States and some of these have found a home within the boundaries of the Presbytery of Minnesota Valleys. Find this presbytery on the map on page 112.

Across the state border from southwestern Minnesota in Sioux Falls, South Dakota, the Presbyterian community has made steps to form a new Presbyterian church in a growing community of Sudanese immigrants who bring their Christian faith with them. Presbyterians in the Presbytery of Minnesota Valleys are learning from their Sioux Falls neighbors how to reach out to and befriend the growing Sudanese population within their own communities. A Partners, Faith, Life and Witness Committee has been created not only to offer hospitality but also to learn the songs, culture, and rich worship heritage of the Sudanese. With pride and joy, the two very different Christian groups can find common ground in our diverse Presbyterian Church.

Word of the **W**eek
Providence

Providence is the care and guidance of God in our lives.

Scripture

"O Lord, let your ear be attentive to the prayer of your servant, and to the prayer of your servants who delight in revering your name" (Nehemiah 1:11).

Recipe

Maandazi (Fried Bread)

Make this fried bread that is eaten in Africa. You'll need an adult to help you with the frying.

Ingredients

2 cups flour
1/4 cup sugar
1/4 tsp. baking soda
1/4 tbs. active dry yeast
3/4 cups water
2 tbs. vegetable oil plus oil for frying

Stir together the flour, sugar, baking soda, and yeast in a mixing bowl. Make a little hole in the middle and pour the water and 2 tbs. oil into the hole. Mix all the ingredients thoroughly. Knead the dough for 15 to 20 minutes. Make 3 balls out of the dough. Use a rolling pin to roll each ball into a circle. The dough should be very thin. Cut each circle into 4 triangles. In a frying pan heat enough oil to cover the bottom of the pan. Fry the dough triangles until they are brown. Eat the bread warm!

MISSION AROUND THE WORLD

Sudan

Both stories this week talk about a country in Africa called Sudan. Look on the map on pages 110–111 and find Sudan. Who are Sudan's neighbors? During the years of civil war, drought, and famine, many Sudanese fled their homes to live in these bordering countries. Now thousands of Sudanese will be returning home in parts of Sudan. After running from gunfire and then living as refugees under terrible conditions, people will return to a home with no schools, no stores, and no streets. The only institution to greet them will be the church. Through all of their experiences, many Sudanese have felt it was only by trusting God that they survived. Now much work must be done to rebuild their lives.

"The spirit of God will not be denied," writes David Dawson, a member of a Presbyterian delegation from the Shenango and Redstone Presbyteries in the United States that visited Sudan. "The Sudanese people are not defeated nor beaten down. In who they are they reflect the image of Christ as a people redeemed by a gracious and loving God." The task of the church in Sudan is challenging but the people trust greatly in God's providence.

Prayer

Dear God, we are thankful for the way you care for all of us. We thank you for how you have watched out for the Sudanese people who have had to leave their homes. Help us to look for and be friends to those who have been shut out by other people. In Jesus' name we pray. Amen.

Women of the Presbyterian Church of Sudan celebrate at their annual gathering.

Giving What You Have

For every sink or tub with a faucet in your home, put 25 cents in the offering plate on Sunday. For every hose you have outside hooked up to running water give 10 cents.

What You Can Do

In Minnesota and in Sudan as well as around the world, Christians are opening their hearts and their homes to newcomers. You too can practice the art of hospitality. Invite some neighbors over for a cup of hot apple cider. Ask them about places they have lived before and what they like best about living in your neighborhood. Even if you know them well, you may learn something new. By practicing hospitality, you will be more able to welcome someone you don't know as well.

Did You Know?

In the United States we can go almost anywhere and get potable water. That means we can drink our water without fear of infection or germs. In many countries people have little or no potable water. It's particularly hard for refugees to find safe water to drink. People must boil their water in order to use it for any drinking or cooking.

Scripture

Great is the LORD's steadfast love toward us, and the faithfulness of the LORD endures forever (Psalm 117:2).

MISSION IN THE UNITED STATES

Presbytery of Northern Waters

Minnesota, Michigan, Wisconsin

What if you had never heard any of the stories of the Bible? How would you know about God's love for all people? How would you know how God wanted us to act toward one another? The members of First Presbyterian Church in Hibbing, Minnesota, knew that many children in the town didn't go to church and probably didn't know about God's great gifts to all of us. After much discussion, the church started an after-school program. The biblical stories of people of faith would be the focus of each session.

Did You Know?

November 1 is All Saints' Day. This is a day when we remember all the people of faith who, in their daily lives, have been models of what it means to be a disciple. On the Sunday of this week many churches read the names of all the members who have died in the past year.

The children in the program spend Wednesday afternoons playing games, studying the Bible, acting out Bible stories, worshiping, singing, and eating together. The games and activities chosen are intentionally cooperative so that all the children feel that their talents can be used. After the fun, caring, and learning on Wednesdays, the children are encouraged to attend Sunday school and worship on Sunday mornings. They are invited to bring friends and family. Children are taught to share God's word as a way of reaching out to include more people in their community.

Puzzle: Saints' Hymn

Collect all the letters with the number 1 to spell the first word on the lines below. Do the same with letters for numbers 2 through 9. After you collect the letters for each number, arrange the letters in their proper order to find the title to this hymn about saints. You can check your answer by looking at #364 in *The Presbyterian Hymnal*. Read the hymn to find out about some important saints.

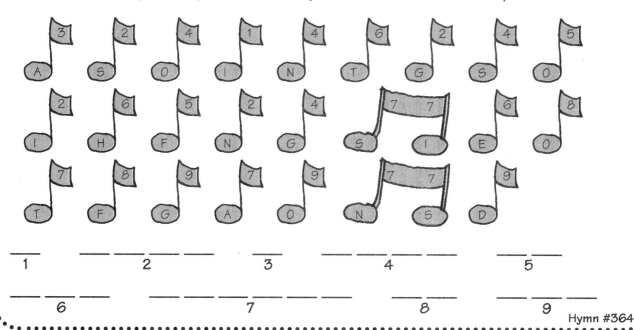

MISSION AROUND THE WORLD

Taiwan

It is said that the native people of Taiwan learned to sing so clearly and with perfect pitch when they would sing from one mountaintop to another to give messages to each other. They would sing to another person to come help them catch a mountain pig. Or they would sing to tell others they were leaving the mountain to come back down into the valley.

When most of the native people became Christians, they brought their singing with them into the churches and began to praise the God who created their beautiful lands in the mountains and on the coast. The native people make up one-third of the churches in the Presbyterian Church in Taiwan, a partner of the PC(USA). Many no longer live in the mountains and along the coast but in cities where they have moved to find work. Now the Presbyterian Church in Taiwan has the job of staying connected with these Christians as they live in new surroundings. Find Taiwan on the map on page 111.

A Lucai tribal choir sings praise to God in Taiwan.

What You Can Do

Become an electric steward and help save the earth! As the weather gets colder many of us crank up the heat in our homes, only to have it disappear through drafts in doors or windows. Ask your parents when the last time they had an energy audit done at your home. Most communities offer a free energy audit once or twice. You can call your local utility company and ask someone there about doing an energy audit in your home.

Word of the Week   Saint

We usually think of a saint as a person who lives an extraordinary Christian life. The New Testament refers to all members of churches who are Christians as saints.

Giving What You Have

Since All Saints' Day is upon us, think of a church school teacher, youth adviser, choir director, or special person in the church whom you look up to. Write that person a short note and explain how he or she has been important to you in your faith.

Prayer

Thank you, God, for the people who show us how to be your followers in the way they live—in the way they listen, smile, do acts of kindness and justice, and show your love by loving others. Help me to find the ways I too can live the life you would have me live. In Jesus' name. Amen.

Scripture

Then Jesus told his disciples, "If any want to become my followers, let them deny themselves and take up their cross and follow me" (Matthew 16:24).

What You Can Do

Find out if your church is collecting food and other items to give to families in need at Thanksgiving. If so decide what you will give.

Giving What You Have

How many theological schools are a part of the PC(USA)? (You can find this information somewhere on page 95.) For each one, put 5 cents in the offering plate on Sunday.

Craft

Masi Cloth Wall Hanging

A traditional craft in Fiji is making things from masi cloth, which is made from the inner bark of the mulberry tree. The bark is soaked in water, scraped with shells, and then pounded into thin sheets with mallets. Historically masi cloth was used for clothing, but today it is used to create beautiful wall hangings and place mats. You can make a similar wall hanging or kitchen mat.

Materials

a piece of parchment paper
newspaper
acrylic paint in bright colors
foam stamps or potatoes cut in half (stamps
   might include a leaf design, geometric
   shapes, or lines and squiggles)
small foam brush
large foam brush
paper plates
a dowel rod 2 inches wider than the
   parchment paper for a wall hanging
clear tape
cord

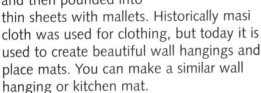

- Prepare a sturdy, hard surface to work on by putting newspaper on a table or on the floor.
- Lay your parchment paper on the newspaper. Position your dowel rod 1/2 inch from the top and centered so there is at least 1 inch on either side of the parchment paper. Roll the top of the paper down over the rod and tape it. Turn the paper over so you can only see 1 inch of the rod on each side of the paper.
- Squeeze a small amount of each color of paint onto separate paper plates.
- If you are using potato halves as your stamp, cut the potatoes in half and have an adult carve a simple design into the white part of the potato half.
- Choose a color and with a foam brush make a border around the paper.
- Decorate your paper with more borders or with lots of stamp prints. You can dip your stamp gently into the paint on the paper plate, or you can use a small foam brush to paint color onto the stamp and then stamp the paper. You can mix colors on a stamp by painting the top half of the stamp one color and the bottom half another color.
- Remember to use lighter colors first and then darker colors on top.
- Let dry thoroughly. For a wall hanging, tie a length of cord to both ends of the dowel rod. Then hang it!

Word of the Week
Theology

Theology is the study of God and religion.

MISSION IN THE UNITED STATES

Presbytery of Central Nebraska

Nebraska

Celeste Keeney, a high school sophomore, decided she wanted to be a part of healing some of the world's wounds. For three years she led the efforts of her youth group and church, First Presbyterian Church in Kearney, Nebraska, to support Operation Christmas Child, a project of an organization called Samaritan's Purse. Through Operation Christmas Child individuals and churches fill shoe boxes with toys, school supplies, hard candy, and other items. Samaritan's Purse ships the boxes to children who are victims of war, famine, or disease in the United States and around the world.

The first year Celeste's church put together 95 boxes to ship. The second year her church was joined by neighboring churches to collect 1,100 boxes. This past year Celeste's leadership helped the churches collect over 4,000 boxes. Celeste was selected to travel to Trinidad to help hand out over 6,000 boxes to children. "At every distribution we did, there was a child who touched my heart," said Celeste. "A particularly awesome experience was when I handed over a box I had filled back in Kearney to a two-and-a-half-year-old girl, Rishma. The joy on her face was life-changing for me."

First Presbyterian Church in Kearney is a part of the Presbytery of Central Nebraska. Find this presbytery on the map on page 112.

MISSION AROUND THE WORLD

Fiji

How do you get to your school each day? Is there a bus that picks you up? Or maybe you are close enough to walk. In Fiji, an island in the Pacific Ocean, the Pacific Theological College Education by Extension, goes to where its students live. (Find Fiji on the map on page 111.)

Located in Suva, the capital of Fiji, Pacific Theological College was founded in 1966 as a college where students in the South Pacific could study theology and religion. More than 20 denominations helped start the school and now continue to support it. Some students live on Suva's campus while they study. But in the last 20 years the school noticed that many students were not able to leave their jobs and families to move to Suva and attend school. So the college created the Education by Extension program, which travels to students. Students are now able to take classes while continuing to work and live with their families. Presently over 200 students are enrolled in the program.

Did You Know?

The PC(USA) has 10 theological seminaries in the United States and has close connections to two others.

The Mission Yearbook for Prayer & Study has a directory of all the seminaries and colleges that are connected with the PC(USA). If you look in Appendix A you will find many wonderful places around the country where students are learning more about the church while they study!

Prayer

One form of prayer is an action that follows the example of Jesus. Today "pray in action" by doing a thoughtful deed for someone without being asked and without expecting something in return. Let your heart pray for that person while you do a secret good deed!

MISSION IN THE UNITED STATES

Presbytery of Lake Huron

Michigan

Jesu sa rang ha simeun
Keoruk hashin mal ilsse
Wu ri deul en yak ha na
Jesu kwonse man to da.

Do you think you know this song? A PC(USA) church in Michigan can tell you that this is a familiar song in English and Korean. "Jesus Loves Me" is only one of the connections churches in the Presbytery of Lake Huron made with their Korean Presbyterian guests during a summer youth exchange program. Twelve young people from Pyung Buk Presbytery in South Korea traveled to Michigan to spend three weeks learning about U.S. culture and the PC(USA). These youth led vacation Bible school, participated in worship, sang, prayed, and shared their faith with their American hosts. The summer exchange program was so successful that many host families are planning visits to their new friends in Korea. And the enthusiasm of the youth from both countries has led the adults to find new ways to further the two presbyteries' partnership in ministry.

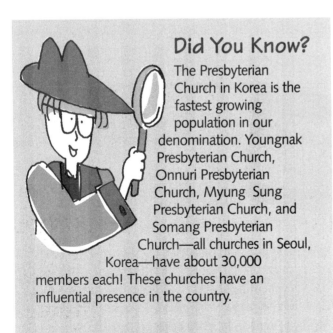

Did You Know?

The Presbyterian Church in Korea is the fastest growing population in our denomination. Youngnak Presbyterian Church, Onnuri Presbyterian Church, Myung Sung Presbyterian Church, and Somang Presbyterian Church—all churches in Seoul, Korea—have about 30,000 members each! These churches have an influential presence in the country.

Scripture

Therefore encourage one another and build up each other, as indeed you are doing (1 Thessalonians 5:11).

Recipe
Cucumber Vegetable Salad (Namul)

Ingredients
3 small cucumbers
1 clove garlic
1/4 tsp. salt
1 tsp. sesame seeds
1 tsp. sesame oil
1/4 tsp. cayenne pepper
1 tsp. sugar

This is a simple cucumber salad that is wonderful as a cool side dish. Small cucumbers work better than large ones. The cucumbers do not require peeling but you may prefer to peel them.

Slice the cucumbers vertically so you have many thin circles. Sprinkle the slices of cucumber with salt and mix well. Let stand for 20–30 minutes. Pour the cucumbers onto a paper towel and gently press out as much water as you can. The less watery the better! Crush the garlic clove and combine it with the cucumber slices. Add the rest of the ingredients and mix well.

You may choose to refrigerate for 30 minutes before serving but this is not necessary.

MISSION AROUND THE WORLD

North Korea

In Sariwon, North Korea, children at a local orphanage are used to the taste of soybean milk! There aren't many milk cows in North Korea, so in partnership with the PC(USA), the Bongsoo Church of North Korea supplies the orphanage with soybeans for milk, as well as grain for breads and cereals, medicines, and clothing. The soymilk helps the children get enough protein so they can grow big and strong. Presbyterian mission workers Art and Sue Kinsler work with the Presbyterian Church in (South) Korea. Every two months Sue takes supplies to the Sariwon orphanage in North Korea. Some of the supplies she takes—aprons and sleepwear—are made by people who are part of the Koinonia Sheltered Workshop, which is located in Seoul, (South) Korea. Koinonia teaches new skills, provides counseling, and offers Bible study to people with disabilities. Because Korea and North Korea have been divided from each other since a war in the 1950s, many Koreans pray that the two countries can be reunified as one country. Sue believes that the Koinonia workshop in (South) Korea offering supplies to the orphanage in North Korea is one small step toward the two Koreas reuniting.

Singing is one way children at the Sariwon Orphanage start the day.

Word of the Week Partnership

Partnership is working together on a common activity to do God's work in the world.

Prayer

Thank God for cows and goats! Think of the ways you enjoy milk—as a drink, as cheese, as butter or in desserts like ice cream. When you give thanks to God for the foods you like, remember all God's creatures who make them possible.

What You Can Do

The Presbyterian Hymnal has several hymns that list Korean verses along with English verses. Look through a hymnal to see how many hymns include Korean verses. What other languages do you find included in the hymnal?

Ye su rul nae ga

Giving What You Have

Heifer Project International assists families around the world by providing them with animals that will help in their survival. Cows and goats are given to families who would benefit from the milk these animals produce. The families can also sell the milk to others as an added income. Find out more about Heifer Project online at www.heiferproject.org and see if your family or your church might help in purchasing a goat or cow for a family in need. You can also read *Beatrice's Goat* by Page McBrier or *Faith the Cow* by Susan Bame Hoover. Both stories illustrate how Heifer Project changes lives.

MISSION IN THE UNITED STATES

Presbytery of Mackinac

Michigan

Imagine . . . you are in church and the music begins. You reach your hand down to get a hymnbook and you find that only half the book is there. You look around at the people in the pews and realize no one has a complete hymnbook. Some people don't even have the hymn you are about to sing. This is what a retired pastor from the Presbytery of Mackinac in Michigan found when she traveled to the Presbyterian Church of Savoonga, which is in Alaska on St. Lawrence Island just 70 miles from Siberia, and is part of the Presbytery of Yukon. As the church sang "Alleluia" on that chilly Easter Sunday, she discovered that every hymnbook was falling apart.

At the next Presbytery of Mackinac meeting after her return to Michigan, the pastor held up one of the tattered hymnals she had used in Alaska. As it fell apart even further in her hands, the presbyters at the meeting responded by making a commitment to purchase over 35 hymnbooks for the Savoonga Church. A partnership between the Presbyteries of Mackinac and Yukon was further strengthened by this gift of song. Find the Presbytery of Mackinac on the map on page 112.

Scripture

Make a joyful noise to the LORD, all the earth. Worship the LORD with gladness; come into the LORD's presence with singing (Psalm 100:1–2).

What You Can Do

Make bookmarks for the hymnals in your church. If your church provides younger children with worship activity bags, the bookmarks could be put in the bags. Or you can slip a bookmark into each hymnal in the pews. Consider making the bookmarks using the church color of the season. Advent starts November 27 and its color is purple. Other church seasonal colors include white, green, and red.

Did You Know?

On the 83 islands of Vanuatu, Presbyterians outnumber any other religious group! The islands have a 36.7 percent Presbyterian population.

Word Puzzle

Find the message by crossing out the unnecessary letters. Hint: There is a pattern to crossing out the letters. Once you think you have the letters, read the sentence and do what it says!

FMQATKOERAPJBOCYEFAUALRNKOPINSUEYTLOVTDHWENLSOXRKD

_____

Answer: Make a joyful noise to the Lord.

MISSION AROUND THE WORLD

Vanuatu

As you approach the low cinderblock buildings, you see rows of coconut trees and hear many soothing sounds. The first sound you hear is the lorikeets (parakeet-like birds) singing in the trees, and then you hear the gentle waves against the reef. Finally you are greeted by the harmonious sounds of children singing. When visitors hear that, they know they have arrived on the campus of Onesua Presbyterian College (OPC), located on one of Vanuatu's islands. See if you can locate Vanuatu (pronounced vah-noo-AH-too) on the map on page 111. Presbyterians in Vanuatu sing to God at every opportunity. Before a church service begins, singing often breaks out spontaneously. Lora and Bruce Whearty, mission co-workers and teachers at

OPC, tell of a Vanuatuan legend about a beach on the island where large stones were lifted and moved by people singing the stones to the spots where they should rest so boats could safely reach the island's shore.

Rosana, a seventh-grade student at Onesua Presbyterian College, sings and keeps rhythm in morning worship.

Prayer

Music is one of the best ways we have to express joy. If you play a musical instrument, play the most joyful song you know as a prayer. If you don't play an instrument, sing the most joyful song you know and use your hands as a drum as you sing. Or you can shout your joy! Think of people, things, and activities that bring you joy. Joyfully and loudly shout your thanks to God!

Word of the Week Joy

Joy is a feeling of delight and happiness. When you experience joy you are very pleased.

Giving What You Have

As a family, visit a nursing home, retirement community, or hospital to sing carols to residents during the Christmas season. You might invite some other families to go along with you!

What two groups of people are supported by the Christmas Joy Offering? Look in the Mission Yearbook for Prayer & Study on page 355 to find out. Ask if your church takes the offering and what you can do to help.

MISSION IN THE UNITED STATES

Presbytery of the Western Reserve

Ohio

Scripture

Our soul waits for the LORD; the LORD is our help and shield (Psalm 33:20).

A church in Ohio wanted to help people who were hungry in their community. Kids in the church said, "We want to help!" Somebody said, "We could collect money and food for the Lend-A-Hand Food Pantry. It serves people who are hungry in our area." And someone else said, "Hey, I know how the kids in the church can help!"

That's how the Rollin' Wheel-a-thon got started. Children riding bikes take part in the fun of helping somebody else. Every year since 1990, First Presbyterian Church in Ashtabula has held a Rollin' Wheel-a-thon. The children of the church invite their friends to join them at the church to ride bikes. All the riders get sponsors to pledge food or money for each lap around the church educational building they make. It's not just bike riders that participate. Children on unicycles, tricycles, roller blades, even babies in strollers go around the building as many times as they can. Often they raise many cases of food and more than $1,000 for the food pantry. And they learn that giving and sharing are the heart of mission and can even be fun. First Church in Ashtabula is in the Presbytery of the Western Reserve. Find this presbytery on the map on page 112.

Craft

Advent Necklace or Key Chain

This necklace will help you count down the days until Christ's birth. You can also use it as a key chain. You'll need an adult to help with the toaster oven.

Materials

1 piece of plastic sheeting, about
   8 1/2 x 11 inches
multi-colored pencils
hole punch
purple, lavender, and white plastic
   pony beads
thin purple ribbon, about 30 inches long
aluminum foil
spatula
oven mitts
toaster oven

☀ Set toaster oven at 300 degrees.
☀ On the plastic sheeting use a black pen to draw a crown and 4 other Advent symbols, such as a star, an angel, a horn, a shepherd's crook, or a sheep. The shapes should be about 3 inches tall—they will shrink when heated. Color the symbols.
☀ Cut out each symbol and punch a hole at the top. (Remember to do this before putting the symbol in the toaster oven. It is impossible to do it afterward.)
☀ Place the symbols on a sheet of aluminum foil folded to fit in the toaster oven. Follow the directions on the plastic sheeting package to cook. It usually takes less than 5 minutes. The symbols will shrink.
☀ After the symbols cool, make a knot in one end of the ribbon and start stringing the necklace. Each symbol will mark a Sunday in Advent, so put a symbol on the ribbon to start. Then, alternating colors, put 6 beads for 6 days of the week on the ribbon. Thread on another symbol to represent the next Sunday. Repeat this pattern of 6 beads and a symbol. Use the crown symbol as your Christmas Day symbol. Once you have finished stringing the symbols and the beads, tie the two ends of the ribbon together to make your necklace. For a key chain, cut off extra ribbon before tying the ends together, leaving enough room for a key.

Children riding bikes in the Rollin' Wheel-a-thon learn to help others while having fun.

MISSION AROUND THE WORLD

Philippines

Can laughter make us stronger? In the Philippines young people try to shake the sadness they feel from unrest in the world by joining together to pray and laugh. In church youth groups, young people gather to study, talk, and pray. They also know the power of laughter. Cobbie Palm, a PC(USA) mission specialist who led a retreat for students, writes, "We lay our heads gently on the stomach of our companion and we look up to the heavens and say, 'Creator God, comfort us; give us your permission to feel goodness so we can live another day.' The Lord gives us laughter and as we feel the laughter of our companion we laugh harder and harder. When we are through laughing, we feel refreshed and hopeful." Laughter does make us stronger. It brings strength to work another day building with God a better tomorrow.

Find the Philippines on the map on page 111.

Silliman University students enjoy each other's company at a spiritual retreat.

Word of the Week — Waiting

Waiting is a time of anticipating, watching, and preparing. In Advent we are preparing our hearts and homes for Christ to enter.

Prayer

Find a place to make a "waiting room." Sit quietly and think about things you wait for: for doctor or dentist appointments, for a new baby to arrive, for someone to come home, for a friend to call. As you think of each of these circumstances, pray: *God, come sit with me while I wait. Help me so I won't worry or be afraid or be impatient. Remind me that wherever I go in life you will be with me. In Jesus' name. Amen.*

Did You Know?

Pre-Christian people in Germany would gather around evergreen branches and fireplaces during the long, cold winters. The scent of the greens and the light of the fires would give them hope for the coming of spring. We keep these traditions alive at Advent as we light candles surrounded by greenery and recognize the birth of Christ as the everlasting light and hope to the world.

What You Can Do

Share the gift of smiles and laughter with your family this week. See if you can start each morning with a smile and a kind word. Try to share God's love with those you meet through laughter. End the day by giving someone you love a hug.

Giving What You Have

How many subjects will you study this week at school? For each subject you study give 25 cents to the Christmas Joy Offering, which your church may be collecting. Ask your church school teacher if the church has ordered coin boxes for the offering. In many churches the offering will be received the Sunday before Christmas, December 18.

MISSION IN THE UNITED STATES

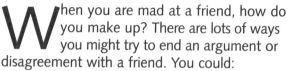

Seattle Presbytery

Washington

When you are mad at a friend, how do you make up? There are lots of ways you might try to end an argument or disagreement with a friend. You could:

☀ Stop being mad.
☀ Forgive the friend in your heart and then tell your friend that you have forgiven him or her.
☀ Call the friend and talk things out.
☀ Go see the friend and hug him or her.
☀ Tell the friend you are sorry.
☀ Let the friend know you still want to be friends.
☀ Forget the argument or disagreement and go back to having fun!

Sometimes people in churches get mad at one another and sometimes churches get mad at the presbytery. Sometimes it can take a long time for forgiveness to take place. It can take a long time for a presbytery or a church body to figure out how to say "sorry." When this does happen, it is called being reconciled or reunited.

In Seattle Presbytery a difficult reconciliation process began between Madrona Presbyterian Church, Mercer Island Presbyterian Church, and the presbytery. On World Communion Sunday a Service of Reconciliation was held. Members of both churches joined their hearts together with members of the presbytery and lifted their prayers to God who offered them all grace. Find Seattle Presbytery on the map on page 112.

Choirs sing during the Service of Reconciliation.

Scripture

Jesus said to him, "'You shall love the Lord your God with all your heart, and with all your soul, and with all your mind.' This is the greatest and first commandment. And a second is like it: 'You shall love your neighbor as yourself'" (Matthew 22:37–39).

Recipe

Australian Oat Cakes

These oat cakes may be similar to the cakes Ibu made for her children to sell.

Ingredients

3 cups flour
3 cups oats
1 1/2 cup butter
1 cup sugar
2 tsp. salt
1 tsp. soda
3/4 cup water

Mix all ingredients together with your fingers until the dough is stiff enough to be rolled. Sift flour on a clean counter or table and roll the dough out on it. The dough should be 1/4 inch thick. Cut the dough into squares and diamonds and bake on a cookie sheet at 350 degrees for 10–15 minutes. Cool the cakes on wire racks.

Word of the Week Reconciliation

Reconciliation is what happens when you bring someone back into your heart and find peace with that person. People are reconciled when they can forgive each other and move beyond the hurt.

Did You Know?

Ambon, the capital of the Maluku islands in Indonesia, has had much fighting between Christians and Muslims since 1999. Though there had been conflict between people of both faiths in previous centuries, a way of relating called *pela*, which means "brotherhood," helped Christians and Muslims in the islands live together peacefully for many years. Christian and Muslim villages would form a *pela*, and they would work together in good times and bad, even helping each other build churches and mosques.

What You Can Do

Help "prepare the way" for Christ's birth by clearing the way. Clear out clutter in a closet in your home or clean up debris in a park near your home or school. Invite some of your church friends to meet you at the church one Saturday morning and scrub the nursery toys and play areas. Cleaning up and clearing out help us to prepare our own hearts to welcome Jesus.

Giving What You Have

Think of a friend or someone in your family with whom you have been angry recently. Pray for that person and pray for yourself. Ask God to help you turn your hearts to forgiveness so that true reconciliation can happen. Why not go to that person and give him or her a hug? Put 25 cents in your Christmas Joy Offering box while offering a prayer for that person.

Prayer

Place something you love and which is breakable on a table in front of you. Think about what it would be like if it were broken. When peace is shattered, God's heart breaks. Pray for peace among all people, thinking of the people and places that are "broken."

MISSION AROUND THE WORLD

Australia

Ibu Eni makes and sells little cakes on the island of Ambon in Indonesia, north of Australia. (Find Australia and Indonesia on the map on page 111.) Her little cakes are made of dough and cooked fresh each morning. In order for Ibu to attend workshops on reconciliation sponsored in part by the Uniting Church in Australia, she had to return home late each evening and prepare the dough for the cakes that her children would then sell before school. She and her family woke early each morning to bake the little cakes and wrap them for sale. These little cakes were the family's only source of income. The workshops Ibu wanted to attend were entitled "Closing the Gap," and they brought together women from Muslim and Christian communities. The Uniting Church in Australia helped set up a house where these women could eat, sleep, and work together for a week. Each person had to put her fears and mistrust of the others' faith and customs behind her. Through the week they began to understand that each could help with the others' burdens. One way of helping became clear when the participants learned of Ibu's reason for leaving each night. They made a plan to purchase all Ibu's cakes each day so her family would be taken care of during her time at the workshop. The women took concrete steps to make their dream of living together in peace possible.

MISSION IN THE UNITED STATES

Olympia Presbytery

Washington

Does your church sing hymns accompanied by an organ or a piano? Or do you sometimes hear bagpipes and harps? Maybe you are used to guitars and electric keyboards? What about rattles and drums? Or saxophones and a blues band? Maybe these are not instruments you would normally hear in your church, but at two churches in Washington State, new songs are being lifted to God with these instruments and are changing people's lives. At the Church of the Indian Fellowship songs of praise have been sung for 100 years using Native American instruments and incorporating Native American symbols and rituals. Now the church has ordained and installed its very first Native American pastor. And at Westminster Presbyterian Church, the Blues Vespers Service brings together people from the church and the community to worship, dance, and sing using the music of the blues to lift their praises. In these two churches in Olympia Presbytery, people inside and outside the Christian tradition find a place to belong. Old traditions give rise to new traditions. Familiar hymns blend with new songs of praise. Find Olympia Presbytery on the map on page 112.

Did You Know?

The name Alaska comes from the Aleut word *Alyeska*, which means "great land." The Aleuts are native people of Alaska. One of the skills the Aleuts are known for is their fine weaving.

Scripture

Rejoice always, pray without ceasing, give thanks in all circumstances; for this is the will of God in Christ Jesus for you (1 Thessalonians 5:16–18).

Craft

Chinese American Christmas Card

Make a Christmas card for a friend or your family using these Chinese words and some English words. You will need good quality, heavy paper that you can fold in half, a small paintbrush, black paint, water for your brush, and other colors of paint or colored pens.

Decide what message you will make by mixing the Chinese words and adding a few English words. Example: I wish you  (Chinese symbol of happiness).

Fold the paper in half, then using the brush and black paint for the Chinese symbol and the other colors for the English words, write your message on the inside of the card. You may want to decorate the outside also.

福
Happiness

愛
Love

和
Harmony

平
Peace

MISSION AROUND THE WORLD

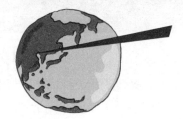

China

The young woman is wearing a brightly colored Chinese jacket. A traditional scarf covers her head. She is kneeling on a mat on the floor, and beside her is a small woven basket with a blanket and pillow inside it. In her arms is a sleeping baby. He too is in brightly colored clothing. He is wearing a little hat with a lion face on it. A small toy rests to the side of the mother and child. The young woman stares at the baby. Maybe it has been a long night and he has been crying. But he looks so peaceful now. Do you know what scene the artist of the painting described here is trying to recreate for us?

Although the scene may not be familiar to us, for children in China this is an image of Mary and the baby Jesus. Just as we might imagine the holy family to look somewhat like our family, the children in China may think that Jesus looks like them! In this picture the artist includes Chinese toys. Rather than a manger in a stable, there is a more traditional Chinese basket bed with a pillow instead of hay. The baby Jesus wears a lion-faced hat for good luck. Looking at this different vision of the Christmas story helps us to see the similarities and the differences of Christians around the world. Recognizing these things helps to bind us together in the Christ child.

Find China on the map on page 111.

Children in China may picture Mary and the baby Jesus differently than children in the United States.

The Synod of Alaska-Northwest's wonderful new logo uses the image of loaves and fishes from the parable in Matthew 14. Find this new logo on the December 23 page in the Mission Yearbook for Prayer & Study.

Prayer

We can pray through song and we can pray through art. What are you thankful for this week? Or what are you concerned about? Draw a picture to show either one. As you draw, offer your thanks or concern to God.

Word of the Week Tradition

A tradition is a custom, practice, or belief handed down from generation to generation of adults to children to grandchildren and so on.

What You Can Do

Make a "good deeds" manger. You'll need a small box and a plastic lunch bag filled with hay, pine straw, or thin strips of paper. Put the box in a central place in the house. Next to the box leave the bag full of hay, pine straw, or paper strips. Let family members know that you are trying to make a soft, full bed for Jesus to lie in when he comes on Christmas Day. The bed can be made softer by adding pieces of hay. But the only way to add bits of hay is to do a good deed for someone else. Each time someone in the family helps someone else, he or she can add a piece of hay. By Christmas Day you will see how your family's good deeds are overflowing.

Giving What You Have

Last week you may have received an offering box for the Christmas Joy Offering. (If you did not receive one, why don't you make one?) For each time you are able to add a piece of hay to the good deeds manger, put 5 cents in the Christmas Joy Offering box. Ask your family to do the same and increase the amount you can give to help support this offering.

Christmas Joy Offering

MISSION IN THE UNITED STATES

Presbytery of Dakota

Nongeographic

Can you remember the time you felt most alone? Imagine not being able to be with your mom or your dad or your grandparents when you are sick. Imagine being a little tiny baby who is sick and has to stay in the hospital without his mom or his dad or any brothers or sisters. The Rev. Dorothy Duquette's (doo-KET) son James was born with a lung condition that kept him in the hospital for the first three months of his life. To make matters worse, the hospital was two hours away from her home and her church. For months she would spend several days at the hospital with James, then drive two hours to her home and spend several days with her family and congregation, then drive back to be with James. It wasn't just tiring; it was getting expensive!

Scripture

Then Mary said, "Here am I, the servant of the Lord; let it be with me according to your word." Then the angel departed from her (Luke 1:38).

Many Presbyterians kept the Duquette family in their prayers for a long time. They also helped with some of the costs. Through gifts to the Christmas Joy Offering, Presbyterians support a program of the Board of Pensions that helps families of church workers who are facing unexpected difficulties. This program not only helps families pay their bills, it also reminds them that they are not facing their problems alone—the family of God is with them both in prayer and in more visible ways too.

The Rev. Dorothy Duquette holds James, her third baby.

Word Puzzle: Mary's Song

Using the following key, decode part of Mary's song of praise to God after she learned that she was chosen to give birth to Jesus.

1	2	3	4	5	6	7	8	9	10	11	12	13	14	15	16	17	18	19	20	21	22	23	24	25	26
A	B	C	D	E	F	G	H	I	J	K	L	M	N	O	P	Q	R	S	T	U	V	W	X	Y	Z

__ __   __ __ __   __ __ __ __ __ __ __   __ __ __ __   __ __ __   __ __ __ __ __ __ __
8 5   8 1 19   2 18 15 21 7 8 20   4 15 23 14   20 8 5   16 15 23 5 18 6 21 12

__ __ __ __   __ __ __ __ __ __   __ __ __ __ __ __ __ __,   __ __ __   __ __ __ __ __ __ __
6 18 15 13   20 8 5 9 18   20 8 18 15 14 5 19,   1 14 4   12 9 6 20 5 4   21 16

__ __ __   __ __ __ __ __;   __ __   __ __ __   __ __ __ __ __ __   __ __ __
20 8 5   12 15 23 12 25;   8 5   8 1 19   6 9 12 12 5 4   20 8 5

__ __ __ __ __ __   __ __ __ __   __ __ __ __   __ __ __ __ __ __,   __ __ __   __ __ __ __
8 21 14 7 18 25   23 9 20 8   7 15 15 4   20 8 9 14 7 19,   1 14 4   19 5 14 20

__ __ __   __ __ __ __   __ __ __ __ __   __ __ __ __ __.
20 8 5   18 9 3 8   1 23 1 25   5 13 16 20 25.

— __ __ __ __   1:52–53
12 21 11 5

MISSION AROUND THE WORLD

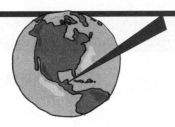

Mexico

Josue (HO-soo-ay) was born in Chiapas (chee-AH-pahs), Mexico. His mother, Janice, was from Michigan and had met his father, Pablo, on a mission trip. Later, Pablo came to study at a seminary in Michigan, and the two met again. When he graduated, he asked her to marry him and join him in ministry in Chiapas. Now Pablo directs a Bible school there, and Janice teaches English and does the cooking for the school. They have very little money, but their life is good.

Josue, called Josh because his name is Spanish for Joshua, was born three years after they moved to Mexico. When he was old enough to go to high school, his parents wanted him to attend Presbyterian Pan American School (PPAS) in Texas. But one year there would cost more than the whole family earned most years, so Josh said no. His mother called PPAS and found out he could attend on a full scholarship if the family could provide his transportation and spending money. This time Josh said yes.

Josh is in his third and final year at PPAS. In addition to studies, Josh runs track, plays soccer, and works two days a week cleaning one of the buildings. He is grateful for the 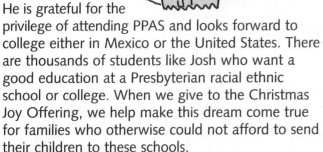 privilege of attending PPAS and looks forward to college either in Mexico or the United States. There are thousands of students like Josh who want a good education at a Presbyterian racial ethnic school or college. When we give to the Christmas Joy Offering, we help make this dream come true for families who otherwise could not afford to send their children to these schools.

What You Can Do

Ask adult members of your congregation if they went to college, where they went, and whether they got some sort of financial aid to help their family pay for their education. You'll be surprised how many did.

Prayer

God of love and mercy, you sent your Son to live among us as a sign and an example of your love, but we didn't really get it, because we were expecting something different. You know we often do that, God—instead of listening to what you tell us through your countless acts of love, we try to fit you into what we want to believe. Help us to understand that what Jesus' life and example offer us, while it may make us uncomfortable, actually is much more wonderful than what we could imagine for ourselves. Open our hearts that we may receive that gift, O God. Amen.

Word of the Week

Grace

Christians use the word grace to mean a kind of blessing that is given to us simply because God loves us. Often we think that by behaving as we think God wants us to, we earn the right to ask God to help us. The Bible tells us that this isn't true; if we got what our behavior had earned, we would have next to nothing. As we get older, many of us learn that there is little we can take for granted as our right; everything valuable is a gift of God's grace. If we train ourselves to look for these blessings or examples of grace, we will begin to become aware of the many ways God uses to reach out to us in love.

Did You Know?

Did you know that gifts to the Christmas Joy Offering enabled the Board of Pensions to help more than 550 families of church workers last year?

Giving What You Have

Probably you are giving thanks every day this week that you do not have to go to school. At the same time each day, think of the millions of children around the world who don't have a good school to go to, give thanks that you do, and put an amount you think is right into your Christmas Joy Offering coin bank.

MISSION IN THE UNITED STATES

Presbytery of North Puget Sound

Washington

Neah Bay is at the most northwestern tip of the contiguous United States. You might think about mountains and crystal clear water, islands, and lots of large trees. And you would be right about all of these. But Neah Bay is best known for being the center of the Makah Tribe's life and livelihood. The Makahs have been in this region for hundreds of years. The name Makah means "generous with food," but the Makahs call themselves Kwih-dich-chuch-ahtx, which means "people who live by the rocks and seagulls." The Makahs are wonderful fishermen. They also rely heavily on products that can be made from the great red cedar trees that grow abundantly. The Makahs continue to teach their children the traditional language, rituals, and crafts.

Amidst this rich heritage sits Neah Bay Presbyterian Church, which is in the Presbytery of North Puget Sound. Can you find the presbytery on the map on page 112? Though it has only 23 members and is located in a remote area of the country, this church reaches out to friends in Russia through a cultural exchange and also to its new neighbors within the community, like Margie Ervine, the church's lay pastor. To be accepted is part of the grace that the members of the Neah Bay church want to extend to others. At an event to mark the anniversary of the death of a young man from the tribe, the new pastor attended as an observer. During the service the congregation called the new pastor forward and wrapped her in a blanket to show their acceptance and respect for her. The Makahs have a saying that if you "see with eyes of wisdom and listen with your heart, time will stand still." Time moves at a different pace in North Puget Sound but the Holy Spirit is still at work.

Scripture

Beloved, since God loved us so much, we also ought to love one another (1 John 4:11).

Recipe

Alaskan Gold

Warm up on a cold morning with this breakfast for your family! This recipe makes 4 servings.

Ingredients

4 slices of bread
4 cups frozen hashbrowns
1 cup chopped onions
4 slices American or
    cheddar cheese

Put a griddle on medium heat. Toast the bread and set aside. Sprinkle 1 cup hashbrowns in each corner of the griddle so you have 4 one-cup piles on your griddle. Sprinkle equal amounts of chopped onion on each pile, then lay a slice of cheese on top of the onions. Let cook until hashbrowns begin to brown and the cheese melts. Do not cover! Using a spatula place each pile of cheesy hashbrowns on a piece of toast.

Recipe from WinterCabin.com

Did You Know?

The Makah Tribe is the only Native American tribe whose right to hunt whales is guaranteed by treaty with the U.S. government. Hunting whales has been a part of the tribe's way of life for centuries, but for a few years the Makahs were not allowed to hunt whales.

MISSION AROUND THE WORLD

Mongolia

What's it like to be an MK, a missionary kid? Esther and Helen Pak are MKs who have lived for more than five years in Ulaanbaatar, Mongolia. (Can you find Mongolia on the map on page 111?) Older sister Esther realized her life would be different from her friends when near the end of her year in second grade, her teacher called her to the front of the class and announced that Esther's family would be "going to the mission field." "That scared me," writes Esther, "because I had no idea what a 'mission field' was. I had thought I was going to Mongolia! I imagined a big, empty grass field. I knew then that my life would not be quite 'normal' again."

When the home church Esther and Helen's parents started grew and moved from their home into a church building, they thought Esther and Helen should do more with the church's children than entertain them and keep them quiet. Their parents wanted the daughters to teach Sunday school. "Sunday school?!" writes Helen. "In a language I wasn't fluent in? I thought it would be hard, but I had a very fun time teaching the kids about the gospel, and while I was teaching them, I got to learn the language. I love the kids just as if they were my siblings. Many MKs come to Mongolia just because of their parents, but I feel like I came to Mongolia not just to be my parents' shadow but to go out and experience being a missionary just like other missionaries."

Esther and Helen Pak are MKs who have lived for more than five years in Ulaanbaatar, Mongolia.

Did You Know?

Sain-bae-no is the Mongolian way of saying "hi." It means "Are you doing well?"

What You Can Do

Offer the gift of hospitality to someone new this week. If you are home on school break, invite a new friend over to your home. Or write a letter to a friend you won't see over the holiday break and tell that friend what you admire or like about him or her.

Word of the Week Acceptance

When we offer people acceptance we receive them as they are. We receive them as a child of God.

Giving What You Have

How many gifts did you accept this Christmas? For every gift you received, put 5 cents in the offering plate on Sunday.

Prayer

Look through your calendar of the year that is ending. Thumb through it to remember people, activities, and events that may have been both happy and challenging. Pray this prayer: *Thank you, God, for the blessings of this year. Thank you too for being near in difficult times and places. In the year ahead bless those in need everywhere in your world. Amen.*

The PC(USA) has mission partners in 6 areas of the world besides the United States.

- Central and West Africa
- Southern and East Africa
- Latin America and the Caribbean
- East Asia and the Pacific
- Central, South, and Southeast Asia
- Middle East and Europe

Russia

onia
atvia
nia
elarus
ep.
Moldova
Ukraine
Bulgaria
Georgia
Armenia
Turkey
s
Syria
estine
em
ypt
Jordan
Iraq
Iran
Kuwait
Saudi Arabia
Oman
Yemen
United Arab Emirates
Eritrea
Bahrain
Somalia
Qatar
Ethiopia
Djibouti
Uganda
Kenya
Burundi
Tanzania
Malawi
Zambia
Zimbabwe
Mozambique
Swaziland
Lesotho

Kazakhstan
Uzbekistan
Kyrgyzstan
Turkmenistan
Tajikistan
Afghanistan
Pakistan
Nepal
India
Bhutan
Bangladesh
Thailand
Maldives
Sri Lanka
Singapore

Mongolia
China
Myanmar
Laos
Cambodia
Vietnam

North Korea
South Korea
Japan

Taiwan
Hong Kong

Brunei
Malaysia

Philippines

Indonesia
East Timor

Papua New Guinea

Marshall Islands

Micronesia
Palau

Nauru
Solomon Islands
Tuvalu
Kiribati
Vanuatu
Samoa
Fiji
Tonga

Seychelles
Islands
Comoros
Islands
Madagascar
Mauritius

Australia

New Zealand

Presbyterian Church (U.S.A.) Synods and Presbyteries

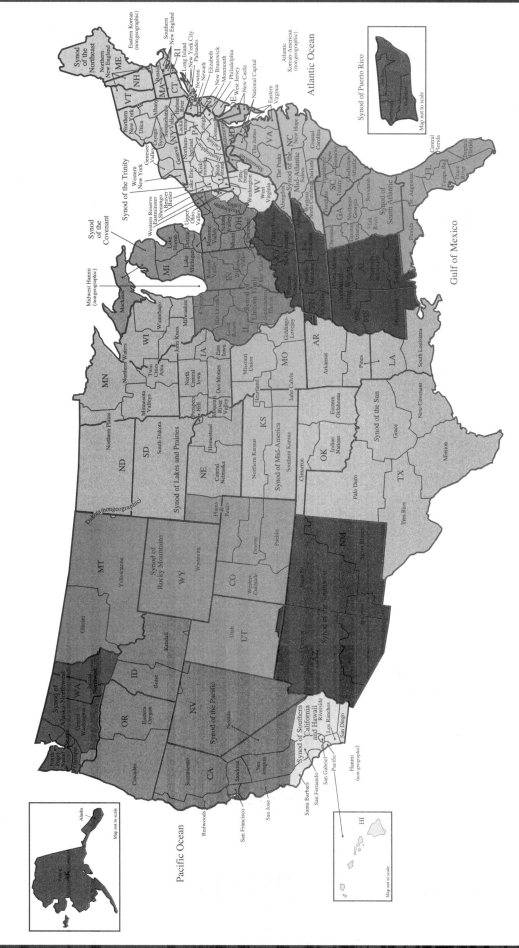